THE PRACTICAL ORGANIC
Gardener

THE PRACTICAL ORGANIC
Gardener

EVERYTHING YOU NEED TO KNOW
WITH MORE THAN 200 ILLUSTRATIONS

Brenda Little

SILVERLEAF
PRESS

Silverleaf Press Books are available exclusively
through Independent Publishers Group.

For details write or telephone
Independent Publishers Group, 814 North Franklin St.
Chicago, IL 60610, (312) 337-0747

Silverleaf Press
8160 South Highland Drive
Sandy, Utah 84093

Contents

"There is great pleasure in working in the soil, apart from the ownership of it. The man who has planted a garden feels that he has done something for the good of the world."

~Charles Dudley Warner, 1870

. . . .

Introduction

Does the name Justus von Leibig mean anything to you? It should, for his ideas have probably affected your life.

He was a scientist and, in 1840, put forward his theory that since the ash of burned plant matter contained only nitrogen, phosphorus and potash they were therefore its only elements. Nitrogen (N), phosphorus (P) and potash (K) became the focus of attention and chemical companies were quick to seize the opportunity to fill what they saw as an obvious need. They could supply NPK. Fertilization by chemical means began and, by the 1850s was becoming established practice. Until then, over the thousands of years men had been growing food on the land, no chemical had been used. The wisdom of Nature had

been noted and acted upon, now it was the turn of
the wisdom of Man.

But Man was not as wise as he thought. Von
Leibig was short-sighted. Without doubt plants
need nitrogen, phosphorus and potash but that is far
from the whole story. What about the rich biological
life in the soil? Trace elements? Mychorrizal effects,
just for starters? So much was overlooked and the
emphasis was wrongly placed. Nature's way is to feed
the soil, not the plants; man's attempt to rely on feeding
the plants while ignoring the needs of the soil went horribly wrong. After some
years the wheat farmers of America were brought face to face with the consequence of their choice. Soil became dead and dry and blew away—nothing would
grow in the desert that remained. The warning was clear. Nature could not be
flouted.

People began to take heed and, fortunately, over the last decades, their number
has grown steadily so that now the basic importance of the health and richness of the
soil is widely recognized. Which is just as well since only about a fifth of the surface of
the earth is covered with soil in which food can be grown and the birth rate continues
to increase.

The evidence of the way we have polluted the planet on which we all depend
for existence has become frightening. The hole in the ozone layer, the death of rivers,

the salinization of land—these problems are too great
for the ordinary man to feel that he has much hope
of correcting, but there is something that can be
done, and more and more people are doing it.

Gone are the days when anyone who advocated organic gardening was considered something of a nut case; now it has become the obvious and sensible method to employ. The folly of the way we have treated the soil has been well demonstrated and the realization that we are ingesting poisons as part of our daily diet is finally coming home to us. Artificial fertilizers, chemical sprays and preservatives all leave toxic residues in the food we eat, and who in their right mind would be willing to continue putting up with that?

The organic gardener can grow his fruit and vegetables secure in the knowledge that he has done the soil no harm and eat them happily, knowing that they are both safe and nutritious.

It all comes back to the health of the soil, a matter of first things first. If the soil is healthy, plants, animals and people all benefit in turn.

Looking after the soil is our sacred trust.

"Man despite his artistic pretensions, his sophistication, and his accomplishments— owes his existence to a six-inch layer of topsoil and the fact that it rains."

~Author Unknown

chapter 1

The Soil

Organic gardeners talk about soil with obsessive love and find deep pleasure in understanding and caring for it. And it's all very simple and natural, and everyone can do it.

WHAT IS THE IDEAL SOIL?

The ideal soil is full of humus and dark in color; the texture is light and crumbly, open enough to let air circulate between the particles. It is pleasant to handle.

It retains water but allows the surplus to drain away easily. It teems with microscopic flora and fauna which we cannot see and is home to many worms which we can see.

The ideal soil has a carbon to nitrogen ratio of 12:1. So what sort of soil do you have?

Testing soil

1. To test for the degree of acidity, collect samples without touching them with your hands.

2. Add the soil carefully to a test tube containing an indicator solution, shake.

3. Compare the color of the shaken solution, after it has settled, with the chart supplied with the kit.

You can also test soil acidity with **litmus paper,** available at most pharmacies.

TESTING SOIL

Soil is unlikely to be the same all over the garden so you will have to make tests in all the strategic spots.

Pick up a handful of soil, moisten it lightly and squeeze it into a ball. If it feels gritty and does not hold its shape but falls apart, it is too sandy. If it feels slimy and can be rolled into a sausage like plasticine, it is too clayey.

IS IT ACID OR ALKALINE? SWEET OR SOUR?

A quick tip-of-the tongue test will tell you if the soil is sour.

A more agreeable way of finding out is to make a litmus paper test. The paper is obtain-able at most pharmacies.

Put a handful of soil into a container and then fill the container with water. Stir the soil vigorously with a stick. When it has settled, drop a piece of litmus paper into the water.

- If it turns blue, your soil is alkaline.
- If it turns pink, it is acid.

If you wish, you can make a very accurate assessment by the use of a pH kit. Any nurseryman will be able to tell you where to get one.

Acidity and alkalinity are measured in pH units. The measurements run from 4—very acid—to 10—highly alkaline. A pH reading of 7 denotes a neutral soil.

Vegetables and herbs like a soil with a pH between 6 and 7. ✕

Most garden flowers and shrubs are happy with a medium acid soil—a reading just below 6 but rarely below 5.5. Azaleas, rhododendrons and camellias are real acid-lovers and can take a reading as low as 4.5.

You can, if you wish, make a few simple corrections before starting your new regimes.

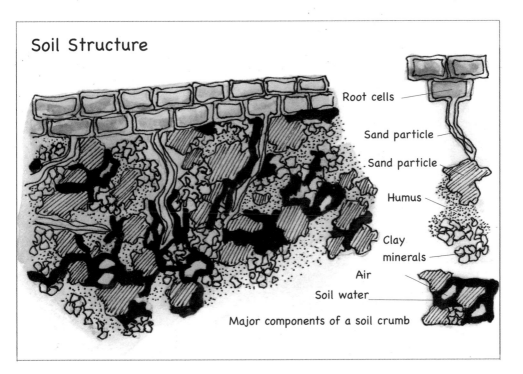

Soil Structure

Root cells

Sand particle

Sand particle

Humus

Clay minerals

Air

Soil water

Major components of a soil crumb

If your soil is too sandy, dig some organic substance into it—leaf mold or old manure.

If it is too clayey, dig some sand and organic material into it.

If the pH reading is below 5, scatter some lime or dolomite over the soil and lightly ruffle it in. If you have to make a correction of more than one point, don't try to do it all at once. Wait a week before making a second application.

If the reading is above 7, work some old cow or sheep manure into the soil. Peat and sawdust will help too. Bring the reading down gradually.

All this is best done while the bed is empty. You will now have some idea of what you have to work with.

Organic gardeners are not enthusiastic diggers. Creating ideal soil on top of soil that is far from ideal and letting things take their course has a far greater appeal. Gardening efforts go into gathering together the ingredients needed to make the mulch and compost, which is so heavily depended upon.

Mulch, compost and humus are the most used words in the organic gardener's lexicon. Some people can be confused as to what's what.

MULCH

The verb "to mulch" means to cover the soil. The purpose is to prevent weed-growth and loss of moisture; to protect plants against the extremes of weather, and mud; and to ensure a flow of air around plants so that they will not become mildewed.

"Mulch" means material used for mulching.

COMPOST

The verb "to compost" means to make a mixture of organic substances that will rot down and turn into humus, which is essential for the fertility of the soil and for favorable moisture content. Humus is the end result of composting. People quite often refer to it as "compost" and this can be a bit confusing. "Humus" and "compost" are not two different things but different ways of referring to the same one.

THE CARBON: NITROGEN RATIO

The ratio needed is one that enables plants to take up food from the soil. Humus has it. It provides immediate food for the plants.

Mulch does not have it. The materials used are usually much higher in carbon than in nitrogen and the soil denizens have to work on it to make the

Preparing your Dirt

1. Dig over the beds with a hoe.

2. Water and fork it over.

3. Sprinkle lime, then add humus.

PEAT MOSS

4. Dig through thoroughly and water.

Soil Texture

You can identify your soil by picking up a handful of moist earth and squeezing—if it breaks into crumbs which feel gritty, it is sandy; if it remains in a solid lump, it's clay.

A clay soil is hard to dig in and drains poorly. A sandy soil will allow movement of air and water but will need extra feeding to retain moisture.

The key is to produce a soil with good crumb structure; clay, silt, sand, and humus particles all need to be present in the correct balance.

conversion, and that takes time. For nourishment from mulch, you have to wait.

Mulch and humus are obviously different but the gardener's need, for one is as great for the other. It is never too soon to start collecting materials from which to make them.

Need for mulch is constant and an organic gardener rapidly becomes an adept scavenger and scrounger and a happy snapper-up of other people's unconsidered trifles. The wider the range of materials the better. Different crops have different needs—the constituents of an ideal soil offer a smorgasbord of nutrients from which they can make their choice.

There are more living organisms in a handful of soil than there are people on earth. That is something to make one think. We take so much for granted and remain unaware of the wonderful complex way that nature works. How much do we understand of the way nematodes, bacteria, fungi, protozoa, myocardial fungi and microarthropods work together and produce a balance in the soil structure which allows water to penetrate but not flood it—and then to retain the correct amount of plants growing in it need—to let in air—to retain nitrogen, potassium, phosphates, calcium, iron and other foods and to release them at a rate which means the plant can absorb them comfortably—to destroy organisms which encourage pests and disease—to break down and decompose plant leftovers? Nature does this with supreme efficiency and we tamper with her methods at our peril. All life on earth depends on healthy soil. Nature should be treated, not as our servant, but out teacher.

The endless cycle of birth and death goes on—nothing is wasted. There is death in the soil—but it becomes life again and the process has been going on since time out of mind. Let us do nothing to interfere with it.

Nature is kind but her patience can run out—organic gardeners recognize this. It is well to remember, as a wise man said, that no matter how intellectual and enterprising man may be, his life is dependent on 6 inches of topsoil and the fact that it rains.

Soil Profile

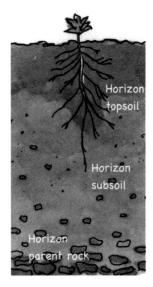

Horizon topsoil

Horizon subsoil

Horizon parent rock

"And what a congress of stinks!
Roots ripe as old bait,
Pulpy stems, rank, silo-rich,
Leaf mold, manure, lime, piled against a
slippery planks,
Nothing would give up life:
Even the dirt kept breathing a small breath."

~Theodore Roethke

. . . .

chapter 2

Compost

The Egyptians and Chinese were using animal manure to fertilize their gardens long before the time of Christ—the Greeks and Romans went one better and mixed the manure with leaves, weeds and food scraps to make a top-dressing for the soil. The idea caught on and by the 15th century Europeans were calling their mixture "compass" or "compost" and the word passed into the English language and the method into practice.

In the 17th century gardeners were writing enthusiastically about the way they prepared their composts and made use of "horse, cattle, sheep, pigeon and poultry dung, ferns, weeds, leaves, food ashes, sticks, sawdust, feathers, hair, horn,

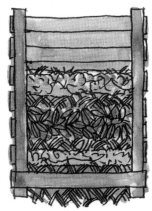

lime
grass cuttings
horse manure
(or straw)
lime
leaves
horse manure
grass cuttings
horse manure

bones, urine, blood, pickle, seawater and the clearing of House and Office"—they didn't let much escape them. If it had once been alive, it was of use.

In the early 19th century scientists began to take an interest in composting and examined the chemical reactions that took place as the mixed materials turned into humus.

In the 1930s Sir Albert Howard, an Englishman, pioneered what became known as the Indore method. He tested his theories in the agricultural region north of Bombay in India—hence the name. His books excited interest, were widely read and became the major influence on the thrust towards organic cultivation.

The methods he advocated remain standard today. His pioneering work was taken up enthusiastically in America, where the folly of chemical fertilization and monoculture were so terrifyingly apparent.

In forests, nature has no trouble in making humus. Leaves and twigs fall, wood rots, little animals and insects die, the forest floor is a mass of decaying substances. But as the substances rot they give nourishment to the soil, which can then feed new plants and animals and from death comes new life. Nature is the original recycler and all we are doing as we make our compost heaps is taking a leaf from her book.

THE BENEFITS OF COMPOST

Compost benefits plant growth.

    1. It supplies for healthy plant growth.

    2. It supplies organisms that suppress disease-causing organisms present in the soil.

Making Leaf Mold Compost

1. If you are a good leaf scavenger, you will have a continual supply of leaves coming in. The easiest way to deal with them is to pile them in a shady spot and water them down.

2. Now sprinkle a light layer of lime over the top of the pile and cover that with a thickish layer of soil. The pile will now probably be about 1 ft. (30 cm) high.

3. Add some blood and bone meal or old, dried manure or some dried chicken pellets. Continue piling and adding manure every 1 ft. (30 cm) until you have a 3 ft. high pile. Leave it to decompose but keep an eye on it to see it doesn't get too wet or dry.

4. When the leaves are nicely rotted, break the pile down and give it a good chopping with a spade, or you could spread the layers out and run the lawn mower backwards and forwards over them a good few times. This will ensure there are no compacted lumps left. Running fingers through any compacted bits and pulling them apart can be quite pleasant.

3. It provides organisms that build structure, allowing water to be retained and nutrients and oxygen to move through it easily. When added to soil, the compost benefits the soil in the same way.

4. Compost contains the organisms that promote plant growth.

5. It has the soil chemistry plants like.

DIFFERENT KINDS OF COMPOST

There are a number of processes by which good compost can be made. In the aerobic approach the compost is made in the open air, left uncovered and turned periodically. The air and heat produced by bacteria create compost. The heat kills weed-seeds and plant-disease-causing organisms.

The anaerobic method employs the use of containers that are covered to exclude air and can stand in the open or under cover. The contents of the bins are not turned.

The third method, worm-composting or vermi-composting, uses earthworms that eat the bacteria in the pile and mix the organic matter promoting the growth of organisms that provide the same nutrient benefits as aerobic compost.

For the lazy or too-busy gardener, the simple throwing of weeds, mowings, spent crops, food scraps into a vacant corner and adding soil and an occasional dollop of fertilizer and letting nature take its course will produce compost in time, but not as good as if care and thought had been taken.

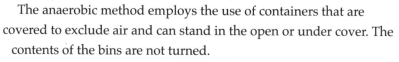

Leaf-mold compost is another option that requires little effort. Good compost should not be allowed to reach too high a temperature, or it will begin to "burn," creating other compounds that can inhibit plant growth.

The compost is "mature" when it has produced the proper set of organisms for the plants and the temperature has reached nearly ambient levels and N-immobilization has been completed. This compost will contain larger numbers of beneficial organisms to benefit plant growth than regular soil will.

STARTING OUT

When starting out, it may be difficult to collect enough material for both mulching and making compost; buying some bales of hay will help out with the mulch and leave more garden refuse for the compost. You can make compost in the open air or in a bin. You can buy excellent bins or, with a little ingenuity, cut down on expense by using an old plastic or galvanized garbage bin from which the bottom has been removed.

The ingredients are garden waste and kitchen waste, some soil and activators such as blood and bone, fish or seaweed emulsion or dried chicken manure. You can also use shredded newspaper, hair clippings, the contents of the vacuum cleaner bag, old woollies, bits of wool carpet—anything that has once been alive.

You can make a small supply of compost in a bucket with holes in the bottom. It is handy if kept outside the kitchen door. Toss the day's kitchen refuse (preferably not meat or fish scraps) and small weeds you pull out while passing through the garden into the bucket (don't forget tea-leaves and coffee grounds) and cover the layer with a mixture of soil and sawdust. When the bucket is filled with alternate layers of scraps and soil, press down well to let excessive moisture drain through the holes, make a top layer of soil, seal the top and put the bucket in a warm, dry place and forget it for a month or two. With luck, when you open it, you will find compost.

The bottom layer must be on the earth and should be loose and coarse, for example, twigs, bracken, corn stalks, etc. The second one is made of garden waste and is about 6 inches (15cm) deep. Sprinkle this with your chosen activator and a very thin layer of earth.

The next layer can be of kitchen scraps but not large bones, which would take forever to break down. If you use them, smash them up. You then continue building up the layers, giving the occasional sprinkling of activator until the bin is full or the heap in the open has reached a comfortable height. It takes time, for the layers sink as they decompose.

The pile should be kept gently moist but never wet so that heat to 122°F (50°C) can be generated. When the pile in the open is finished, you will have to cover it with a thick layer of earth or old blankets to keep the heat in.

The compost will be ready for use when it is loose and black and shows no sign of its original ingredients. The C:N ratio should be at least 10:1. It is better if it is higher.

MATERIALS FOR COMPOST

Garden Refuse

Weeds, before they go to seed
Spent plants
Green leaves
Dried leaves
Bracken
Lawn mowings
Dried stalks
Thin twigs and branches

Hay

Straw

Dead mice and birds

Determined weeds, like oxalis, tradescantia, onion grass, convolvulus and ground elder should be left to dry in the sun before inclusion in the heap. Couch and kikuyu grass runners should be chopped and left to dry out before use.

Diseased plants should not be used. It is too risky. The heat generated might not be hot enough to kill the disease-causing organisms.

Kitchen Waste

Fruit and vegetable peelings

Fruit and vegetables (not fruit fly infected)

Tea leaves, tea bags, coffee grounds

Nutshells, crushed

Oyster and mussel shells, crushed

House Refuse

Vacuum bag contents

Dog and cat combings

Human hair, but not chemically treated

Feathers

Old wool sweaters and old wool carpet

Old cotton garments and sheets

Newspaper

Old letters, bills, envelopes

Urine—which must only be used diluted and after standing for 24 hours.

Other Material
Sawdust
Seaweed

Animal Manure
Cow, horse, sheep, pig, rabbit, goat, chicken, pigeon.

When making your choice of which manure to use, it will help to know that horse and chicken manures contain more nitrogen than the others and pig manure takes quite a time to break down.

ACTIVATORS

Blood and bone meal, fish and seaweed emulsion, dried chicken pellets all help to increase the rate of decomposition of the compost material; comfrey and yarrow are often grown for the specific purpose. It is impossible to speak too highly of the usefulness of comfrey as a medical herb or of its food value to other plants. Yarrow, which contains nitrogen, phosphorus and copper is also valuable. It is said that even one leaf added to each layer you put in the compost heap will speed the breakdown.

Chamomile, the "herb doctor", will keep the heap from going "off" and nettles and dandelion will provide it with iron, copper, calcium, potassium, sulfur—and if you want, iron and manganese too, add chickweed, you're sure to be able to find some growing in the lawn.

AEROBIC COMPOST

Aerobic compost is made in the open air and relies on oxygen and heat for continuing decomposition of the contents. This involves regular turning.

The making of the heap can be as simple or as labor intensive as the gardener feels inclined, but whatever the method used, the principle is the same and if it is not followed, the end result could be a pile of rubbish full of slaters and cockroaches and not brown, crumbly, sweet-smelling humus.

A compost heap is built with the intention of speeding up the rate of decay of the contents by encouraging the activity of a range of bacteria, which break down organic matter. A well-made heap is a scene of frantic activity; the process is involved, but follows a clear pattern.

When the heap is first made, a certain type of bacteria sets to work to break down the con-tents into a simple form. As they work, they create heat. The heat builds and becomes too much for them to endure and they die. A second type of bacteria then takes over and breaks down the material into an even simpler form. The heat rises as they work and when it reaches 122°F (50°C) they, in their turn, succumb and die.

The next lot of bacteria to take over are aptly named thermophiles—they can work at temperatures uncomfortable to the human touch. They go through the pile at a furious pace until everything in it is digested and there is no food left for them. They die and the heap begins to cool down. When it is cool

WARNING:

Do NOT use dog or cat droppings. Domestic pets are not vegetarian and their feces, like human feces, which are also undesirable, contain germs which the heat of compost cannot destroy.

WARNING:

Raw fish and meat scraps, plate scraps, dairy food like sour milk or stale cheese are likely to attract vermin so are unsuitable for the aerobic pile. While they are out of reach of vermin in the sealed bins and bags, the danger from pathogens remains, as it is uncertain whether the heat generated will be enough to destroy them.

enough, worms, centipedes, and millipedes make their appearance and you have humus.

RULES FOR A SUCCESSFUL COMPOST HEAP

1. An aerobic heap must stand on soil.

2. The "mix" should include balanced quantities of green and dried material with an added mixture of manure to encourage decomposition.

It is important to get the C:N ratio somewhere near right.

Think of nitrogen-rich material as being green, fresh and sappy, and carbon-rich as being dried brown and stringy and you won't go far wrong.

3. If you have too much nitrogenous material, the heap will become slimy and smelly. If you have too much carbonaceous material, the heap won't warm up well enough for decomposition to take place.

4. Layers of material should be no more than 6-8 inches (15-20cm) deep.

5. The moisture content of the heap should be more than 40% but less than 60%.

6. An aerobic heap needs to be well aerated.

7. An aerobic heap should achieve an internal temperature of 122°F (50°C).

8. When adding an activator such as blood and bone meal or dried chicken pellets, work on a ratio of 5-7 ounces (150-200g) per 11 sq feet (1sqm).

9. The completed aerobic heap must be protected against weather.

A SIMPLE AEROBIC COMPOST HEAP

1. The bottom layer, which is laid directly on to the soil should be made from loose, coarse material, such as twigs, bracken, dried corn stalks, bamboo stems cut to size. A good idea is to place a couple of bricks under the pile to assist drainage.

2. The second layer is made from a mixture of green waste, garden and kitchen—chopped and mixed and spread over the pile no more than about 6 inches (15cm) deep.

It is necessary to be particularly careful when using lawn mowings. They are fine if used lightly and mixed with other material, but will form a layer impervious to air if laid down too thickly. This is the nitrogen layer.

3. The third layer, of dead leaves, dried stalks, some straw, shredded twigs, crumpled or shredded newspaper, contents of the vacuum bag, etc. will add carbon, and being drier than the previous layer will sop up any excess moisture.

A Simple Aerobic Compost Heap

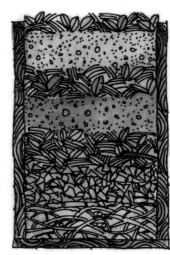

soil, dried blood

dead leaves

soil, dried blood

dead leaves

green waste

twigs

Many herbs make good additions to a compost heap.

4. The pile should now be scattered with a layer of soil combined with some dried manure or some dried blood and bone meal or dried chicken pellets.

It is not necessary to be hard and fast in how you put down the layers—what is important is the keeping up of a mix of ingredients and supplying enough manure to get decomposition under way.

5. Continue making the layers and turn the heap every 5 or 6 days. Some people do it more often, but turning allows heat to escape and if you do it too often, the process under way is slowed down. You can, of course, as mentioned previously, not turn it at all, but give it a good poke and stir instead.

6. Make certain to keep the heap moist but not soggy. It should feel a bit like a wrung-out washcloth.

7. When the heap is about 3 feet (1m) high, cover it up to protect it against the weather. You can wrap old blankets around it or cover it completely with a thick layer of soil.

Forget about it for 8 weeks and then open it up to see how things have gone. If you can't identify the individual ingredients and all you have is a dark brown, crumbly, pleasant-smelling substance, you have succeeded in creating humus.

If it isn't like that, give it a stir, add some blood and bone meal and cover it up again and wait for another few weeks.

WHAT CAN GO WRONG?

Problem: After a week, or even less, the heap is just "sitting" and feels cool. It should start to warm up in about three days.

Solution: You need nitrogen "starter" material.

Introduce some dried chicken pellets or blood and bone meal into the pile. Comfrey, yarrow and chamomile also make good starters.

If you have enough herbs growing naturally, pick a handful or two, soak until limp and add to the pile. Otherwise, use the dried herb to make "tea" and water the pile with it.

Urine is high in nitrogen and can be used as an activator if it is diluted and left to stand for a couple of days before use.

Check to make certain you are keeping the pile slightly moist.

Problem: The pile smells "off."
Solution: It needs more air or it is too moist.

You have let the materials compact either by hard-packing the layers, adding a too-thick layer of a dense material, or by not being careful to see that there is a mix of coarse and fine material throughout.

Do what you can to lighten the material and then sprinkle a teaspoonful of permanganate of potash (Condy's crystals) over the surface and water lightly. Or sprinkle lime over it.

Problem: The pile reeks of ammonia.
Solution: You have used too much animal manure. Add some straw.

Nitrogen and Carbon Sources

*Green leaves, grass mowings, fresh weeds, fruit and vegetable peelings are nitrogen-rich.

*Manure from animals which feed on grass is nitrogen-rich too.

*Dried leaves, dead leaves, dried stems, stalks and branches, straw, sawdust and woodchips are carbon-rich.

Problem: The pile smells musty and there are signs of mold.

Solution: The bacteria are dying off because you have let the pile become too wet and short of air. Use a strong stick to prod and turn it in order to introduce air into it.

Add scrunched up newspaper to sop up moisture and give it a dusting of lime to sweeten it. Then roll up some chicken wire to make a cylindrical "chimney stack" and push it well down into the center of the pile.

Problem: Mice are nesting in the heap

Solution: The presence of mice is a sure sign the heap is not heating properly.

A well-constructed heap will reach about 122°F (50°C) in the center. It becomes too hot for even the bacteria working in it to live, so a mouse would have a little chance of survival.

Check your methods and make sure you are getting the C:N ratio right and that there is enough nitrogen in the heap to get decomposition going. Add some dried chicken pellets or some blood and bone meal to make certain.

Problem: Flies continually hover round the pile

Solution: Tiny compost flies are quite usual, but bigger ones and blowflies mean that you are not covering food scraps well enough.

Don't put cooked food in the pile. Make certain all food scraps are buried deep in the center of the pile. Make certain you don't have too much damp straw around.

After every addition, cover the pile with soil.

Another way of creating humus—but not on the same scale—is vermi-culture, worm-farming.

MATCHING COMPOST TO PLANTS

For ideal results, your compost should match the needs of the particular plants in your garden. For example, if you are putting compost around trees, the organisms in the compost should be beneficial to trees.

VEGETABLES AND LAWNS

Vegetables and lawns do best in bacteria dominated soils. The bacteria produce "slime layers" around their bodies, which glues them to the soil. Because they can't be washed away, the nutrients are retained in the soil. In addition nematodes and protozoa eat them, releasing ammonia into the soil. Other bacteria convert the ammonium to nitrate, the preferred form of nitrogen for vegetables and grasses.

TREES, SHRUBS AND PERENNIALS

Fungal dominated soils suit these plants best.

Fungi produce organic acids as waste. When eaten by predators such as nematodes and fungal-feeding organisms, they release nitrogen in the form of ammonium. Trees and shrubs and many perennial plants grow more efficiently when using ammonium instead of nitrate.

In forests, the inorganic nitrogen is dominated by ammonium while on grasslands, it is dominated by nitrate.

These are optimal conditions and do not mean that plants will not do very well in less than optimal situations.

A BASIC BACTERIAL STARTING RECIPE

For a bacterial compost start with:

1. 25% high nitrogen material such as alfalfa or manure. If the manure is wet, stinky or runny, either avoid it or reduce the percentage to 10% and increase the green and woody material to make up the difference.

2. 50% green leafy material

3. 25% woody, brown, dry leaf, straw, hay, bark materials

A BASIC FUNGAL STARTING RECIPE

For fungal compost start with:

1. 5-10% high nitrogen such as alfalfa or manure

2. 45-50% green leafy material

3. 40-50% woody, brown, dry leaf, straw, hay, bark materials

By trial-and-error you will be able to improve upon these recipes. By increasing or decreasing the percentage of the various ingredients you will find a recipe that works well for you.

COMPOST BINS

Traditional Bins

A wall or strong fence can be used as a backing for these bins. Sheets of corrugated iron or slatted wood make the "walls."

The object is to have a series of three bins, open at the front and of equal size: 22 square feet (2 meters square) and 3 feet (1m) high will do very well.

It is important that air should circulate freely around the heaps so, if using slatted wood, fix the slats at least 2 inches (5cm) apart.

If you use solid sheets of corrugated iron, don't pile material right up to the walls.

The first compartment is used for the storing of material as it becomes available. The second contains a mix of materials in the process of being composted. Materials from the first bin are continually being added to the second bin. After a time, the contents of the second bin are tossed into the third bin with the top layer becoming the bottom

Traditional Bin

one in the new bin.

After a few weeks they are tossed back again and more material from the first bin is added. The turning goes on until the material in the third bin is recognizably humus.

If you have the space and large amounts of degradable material available, you could extend the number of bins, but that is deluxe composting, labor-intensive and beyond the scope of most of us.

The Bocking Box Container

This is one of the simplest and cheapest ways of making a holder for compost. All you need are four strong, 3-foot (1m) high wooden stakes, a roll of chicken wire 3 feet (1m) high and some galvanized nails.

1. Drive the stakes into the dirt to make 11 square feet (1 square meter).

2. Nail or staple one end of the wire to the outside of the first post, then take it round the outside of the next two, fastening it as you go.

3. Make a second run fastening the wire to the inside of the posts. You will now have a gap between the two lots of wire on three sides.

4. Fill this, neatly and solidly with newspaper—

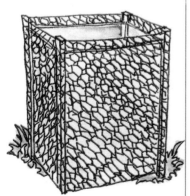

Bocking Box Container

not shredded but left in
the sheet.

5. The front of the box remains
open so you will have to make a "gate"—use wire.

You will probably need a hammer to make the
shape. The gate should be 6-8 inches (15-20cm) less
than the height of the box so that, when it is fixed,
air can reach the pile inside, much as it does in a fire
grate.

6. Measure the width, allowing for the side joins
and fold the wire to fit and do this four times so that
you have a space between the layers—two on each
side, as you have in the rest of the box, which can be
stuffed with newspaper too. Staple or nail into place
across the front of the box, leaving space at the bottom.

The newspaper will help to keep the heat
generated in the pile and can be replaced as it rots.

7. It is important to ensure that the gap at
the bottom of the gate is kept free so that air can
reach the bacteria and keep them working. An
old poker or iron bar kept handy will prove very
useful.

8. The bottom layer should be of loose
twigs and tough stems,
crushed, loose bracken,
etc. Then the box can be

Helpful Hints:

If you are composting with
a pile rather than a bin,
bigger is often better, as
heat builds with size. But
don't get much bigger than
3 feet by 3 feet.

WARNING:

Worms can only be introduced into an anaerobic bin. The heat in an aerobic heap would kill them.

filled, in layers, as for the simple heap. You probably won't have enough to fill it right up at once and will have to keep adding layer after layer until you do.

9. A wooden lid, or one made from tough PVC or corrugated iron will protect against heavy rain—you can take it on or off as needed.

The heap obviously cannot be turned. If you think it needs more aeration, make a little "chimney-stack" by rolling chicken-wire into a cylinder about the circumference of a small, clenched fist and long enough to reach deep into the bin and poke that well down into it.

Other Ideas

1. On a bare soil form old bricks into a square—11 sq feet (1sqm) will be fine. Build the bricks up to 3 feet (1m) high, leaving gaps in the construction for air holes and to allow any surplus water to escape.

The layers should be built up as previously described and kept nice and flat.

No food scraps should go into this bin.

2. Find an old incinerator. With the hole at the bottom and the lid for the top for giving protection against the weather when needed, the old thing is perfect for the job.

ANAEROBIC COMPOSTING

Lazy gardeners will be content to throw their weeds mowings, prunings, spent crops, kitchen and house waste into a vacant corner and just let nature take its course. The pile will rot down of course, and after a wait, compost will be the end result. However, the humus is unlikely to be as good as it should be.

Good anaerobic compost is made in bins or bags that are sealed from the air. The bacteria, which work without oxygen, are different from the ones which work in an aerobic heap and they create a real stink but no heat. This is one of the reasons why anaerobic composting is better done in one go. If possible, materials should be gathered in readiness for the bag or bin and once the filling is complete, the container should be kept sealed until decomposition within it is complete and all that is left is humus.

Anaerobic composting is within the capacity of almost everyone. There is no reason why the owner of a townhouse with a small garden bed in a tiled backyard should not have a personal supply of humus.

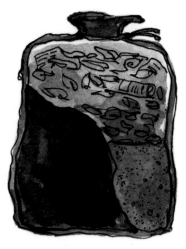

Method One

1. One third fill a heavy-duty garbage bag with soil.

2. Fill the next third of the bag with a mixture of food scraps, mainly fruit and vegetable peelings, limp weeds, shredded

cabbage leaves, green leaves, etc. and then fill it to the top with dead leaves, bits of cardboard, shredded paper, straw, etc. Drizzle water over the contents carefully and make the contents just damp but not soggy and then tie up the top of the bag very tightly and carefully so that all air is excluded and there is no possibility of any getting in. Enclose in another bag for safety and tie that up tightly too.

Method Two

You will need a garbage bin—plastic, aluminum or galvanized. Plastic bins are easiest to handle but can crack after exposure to sunlight.

1. Punch or drill ½ inch (10mm) holes in the bottom and sides of the bin. A good few in the bottom, not so many in the sides.

2. Arrange a stand for the bin. It could be a wad of cardboard or newspapers or bricks and a tray. The base is needed because the bin will leak.

3. When the card or newspaper becomes sodden, tear it up, add to the contents of the bin and substitute a fresh layer.

4. Place the bin in position and put down the bottom layer of material—twigs, crushed bracken, straw, fibrous stalks.

5. Cover with 6-8 inch (15-20cm) soil.

6. Now you can begin adding layers of chopped green material and house and kitchen waste, remembering that anything green and moist will hold nitrogen and anything brown and dryish, carbon. If the mixture seems too wet, dry it by adding a little sawdust. Since this will be acid, sweeten with pulverized eggshells.

Don't pack the layers down tightly and separate them every now and then with some straw mixed with old dried manure or some good soil. If you don't have dried manure add some blood and bone meal or some dried chicken pellets.

While it is best to fill the bin at one go, this is not always possible. If you have to fill it gradually, work quickly each time you make an addition and close the lid as soon as possible.

Method Three

If you have some bare soil on which a bin could stand, cut out the bottom of a plastic, aluminum or galvanized garbage bin and place it, level and firm, in a shady, accessible spot.

You can then fill it in the usual way and leave for about 8 weeks. Inspection from time to time can be done carefully and if the contents are sinking rapidly, more can be added. But do work quickly.

"MADE FOR THE PURPOSE" BINS

The Gedye bin has, for some years, been at the top of the market. It is a large bin made from high-density polythyrene and has a well-fitting lid. The bin, which is open at the bottom is placed directly on the soil, and is filled, in layers, according to accepted practice. It is good looking and efficient, but since it is large, will take time to fill and the bottom layers may have turned to humus while the top layers are still fresh.

This means the bin must be tipped and the humus scraped out or, the luxury way, use two bins and fork out the top layers to make the bottom layers of the second one.

A more recent product on the market addresses this problem.

This bin is separated into two compartments by a perforated screen and is opened from the sides, not the top. The detachable sides are easy to remove and enable you to remove half the compost while leaving the other half undisturbed.

If earthworms are introduced into one compartment, they will work their way through the contents and then find their way through the perforated screen to the materials on the other side.

Look out too for a contraption like the ones used in supermarkets to hold plastic bags in which to take away one's purchases. A bag held open in place is much easier to fill with compost material than if you held the bag in one hand and tried to stuff it full with the other.

Gedye Bin

Another system, involving a heavy-duty, bottomless, lidded, polythyrene bag supported and held in position over bare soil by steel rings and aluminum bars, is like a lightweight Gedye bin. The bag is filled in the usual way with layers of organic material, fertilizer is added, the contents watered and the lid put firmly in place. The contents will have broken down in about two months—the bag can then be lifted off the pile like a bucket being lifted from a sandcastle.

It is worthwhile keeping an eye on the market, for the interest in organic gardening is growing and people with bright ideas are continually coming forward.

Tumbler Bins

These lightweight bins are balanced on a framework so that, at a touch of the finger, they revolve and tumble their contents around—another way of avoiding turning by hand.

They are not overly expensive and—if you have an embarrassment of material—are invaluable, for they have to be full to perform at their best. All material must be neatly shredded. If you don't have a lot of material, this could be a drawback.

Like a shredder, the machine can clog if it is supplied with too much sappy green material and you have to keep an eye on it to avoid excess water. Weeds, grass mowings, fresh leaves are better left to dry and wilt before inclusion.

If the mixture does become too wet, add some straw or sawdust, and a handful of crushed eggshells to keep the acid in the carbon-rich materials down.

The bin should be turned several times a day.

Warning:

Never feed your worms dairy or meat products. And, before you put food in the bin, chop it into tiny pieces to speed decomposition.

VERMI-COMPOST

The worm is the gardener's best friend. Its body which seems so soft and pliant can burrow deep into hard-packed soil, turning and aerating it like a little plough, so that the soil is lighter and easier for plant roots to penetrate and so that water retention and drainage are facilitated.

They digest decayed plant material, clay, sand, bacteria, insect larvae, nematodes and fungi, retain what they need and pass the rest out through their body. Their "castings" are rich in potassium, nitrogen, manganese, calcium, molybendium, all in a form plants find easy to digest and much richer in nutrients than the food they ingested. How they do it is a miracle of nature, which I don't think has yet been conclusively explained and the suppositions are too lengthy and complex to go into in this book. All we need to do is feel grateful and to be certain not to use chemical fertilizers and pesticides which will kill them off. Worms can turn out their own body weight in "castings" in one day and triple their number in about six months. The work they do is one of the most important in the whole ecosystem.

Breeding Worms

You can breed worms in the garden or in boxes, which can be kept on a patio or balcony. The best worms to use are red worms or tiger worms—manure worms they are called and are readily available in most garden centers.

Earthworms are bisexual and each sex can produce an egg-capsule every ten days or so. The eggs take three

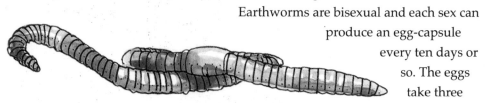

weeks to hatch and begin to mate when they about 3-months-old, and continue to do so every week of their lives—about 2 years.

Visit the box, which should be kept in a shady place every week to sprinkle it with just enough water to keep it damp and leave the worms to breed. They will have eaten their way through their bedding in about 6-8 weeks. Then introduce them to the garden.

Composting with Worms in the Garden

The important thing to remember is that heat is not used in the way it is in other composting methods where it is needed to destroy pathogens and weed-seeds. The worm's digestive system does this for us. Heat above 77°F (25°C) can kill them—they like moist cool conditions.

Start off by making a mix of green and brown plant material—the green parts of the plant and the dry brown ones such as dried stems and stalks cut into pieces, hay and straw—and leave it to heat up in a shady part of the garden. Check to see that the pH is as neutral as possible—worms don't like acid conditions. Add a touch of lime or wood-ash to correct the balance if necessary. After a couple of months, the heating-up process should be over and the temperature of the pile just what the worms like.

What do I feed my worms?
Food scraps of fruits and vegetables, egg shells, tea and coffee grounds.

How big should my container be?
Surface area of 10 square feet for every lb. of food waste weekly.

How many worms do I need?
For 1 lb. of food waste per day, use 2 lbs. of worms.

Now you can put the worms in. Start with a good handful. Tuck food scraps into different parts of the pile to get them going, moisten the pile gently, cover it— gently again so that the air can get to it but light is excluded— worms will only work in the dark.

Once they settle in, they will make an excellent job of disposing of their bedding, so keep up a regular supply of mixed plant material and food scraps. Worms have a voracious appetite and enjoy chopped fruit and vegetables and their rinds, bits of bread and cake, chopped leftover pasta, coffee grounds, tea leaves, teabags, ground rice, cracked wheat, but they don't like fish, meat scraps, cheese or the oily leftovers from a salad. Feed them moderately and regularly and offer them variety.

Variety is important for different plants have different needs and it is good to make their choice as wide as possible. You don't have to do anything—the worms will do it for you and turn everything you provide them with into light friable soil.

Worm Compost Bins

Container

Wood or plastic containers work well and you can either buy them or build them. Use your imagination and recycle an old trunk or drawer. Wood does tend to be better because it is more absorbent and a better insulation for the worms. A polystyrene fruit box—perforated at the bottom—makes a good bin.

Depending on the size of the container, you need to drill 8 to 12 holes in the bottom for aeration and drainage. A plastic bin may need more drainage—if the contents get too wet, drill more holes. Raise the bin on bricks, and place a tray underneath to capture excess liquid, which can be used as a liquid plant fertilizer.

The bin needs to be covered to conserve moisture and provide darkness for the worms. If the bin is outdoors, a solid lid is preferable, to keep out unwanted scavengers and rain. Worms need air to live, so make sure they have sufficient ventilation.

Bedding

It is necessary to provide a damp bedding for the worms to live in, and to bury food waste in. Suitable bedding materials are shredded

10 Points to Remember

1. You must use Red worms or Tiger worms.

2. Chop materials to no bigger than 1 inch, otherwise the worms will have to wait for fungi to reduce the size.

3. Don't let the materials become too wet or too dry. It are too wet if you can squeeze water from the material, and it is too dry if you can blow dust from it.

4. When the worm compost is ready, give it a good mix. This will help control fungi.

5. Only put in 1 1/2 lbs. of food per 10 square feet of space a week.

6. If the compost becomes juicy because of green waste, use torn pieces of newspaper or sawdust to sop it up.

7. Watch the compost to see how the worms are doing. They work just under the top layer.

8. Reduce food as the weather cools.

9. Worms don't work in cold weather. They will burrow down and wait there until warmer weather. Bins should be brought inside when the temperature drops below 53 F (12 C).

10. Vermicompost does not need turning—the worms do all that is necessary.

Water and Soil Type

As water is added to soil, the first 2 to 3 inches (5–6cm) of soil must become very wet before the water can move to the next 2 to 3 inches. Short waterings wet the top few inches but don't dampen the soil below it.

Knowledge of your soil will help you water properly. Sandy soils have large pores and dry out quickly, they need to be watered more frequently. Clay soils have small pores and dry out slowly. It is easy to overwater clay soils, filling the pores and keeping the sun out.

newspaper and cardboard, shredded autumn leaves, chopped up straw and other dead plants, seaweed, sawdust, peat moss, compost and aged manure. Try to vary the bedding in the bin as much as possible, to provide more nutrients for the worms, and to create a richer compost. Add a couple of handfuls of sand or soil to provide necessary grit for the worm's digestion of food.

Method

1. Place a thick layer of chopped newspaper in the box and cover with a thin layer of dry lawn-grass clippings.

2. Add a good depth of compost made from a mixture of one part each old, dried crumbled manure, soaked and squeezed-out peat moss, sieved soil, a good scattering of cornmeal and 4 cups of dried, used coffee-grounds. Mix well.

3. Add a little water to make the mixture hold together. It should not drip but the materials must be moistened so that the overall moisture level is like a wrung-out sponge.

4. The bin should be about three-quarters full of moistened bedding. Lift the bedding gently to create air spaces, which help to control odors and give freer movement to the worms.

Let it stand for about a week, checking it each day for heat. It must be quite cool before you put in your worms.

5. Cover them with a mixture of a 1 to 3 mixture of cornmeal and dried, used coffee grounds and put a thinnish layer of dry grass mowings over that and, finally, a piece of damp sacking—if indoors.

Where Should I Locate the Bin?

Worm bins can be used indoors all year round, and outdoors during milder months or in mild climates. The advantage of a mobile bin is that it can be moved when the weather conditions change. Indoors any spare space can be utilized, so long as the temperatures remain mild. Outside, bins can be kept in sheds, garages, on balconies or in the yard, but they must be kept out of hot sun and heavy rain.

What do I Feed the Worms?

You can compost food waste and scraps such as fruit and vegetable peels, tea bags and coffee grounds. As long as you don't include dairy products, meats and oily foods—they attract flies and vermin—you can recycle all your kitchen waste.

To avoid smells and fly problems always bury the food waste by pulling aside some of the bedding, dumping the waste, and then covering it up again with the bedding. Bury successive loads in different locations in the bin.

How do I Maintain the Bin

If you have the correct ratio of surface area of worms to food scraps, there is little to do, other than adding food, until about two and a half months have passed. By then there should

The Earthworm

"Earthworms have no teeth, so they coat their food with saliva to aid digestion. The leaves and soil enter the earthworm through its mouth and end up in an area known as a gizzard. Within the gizzard, the food is ground up with the help of tiny stones.... As the earthworm travels through the soil digging, eating, and digesting, it actually improves the quality of the soil. Its waste material, called 'castings,' contain valuable nutrients. The nutrients contained in the castings are one of nature's most valuable fertilizers."

—The Alien Earth

be little or no original bedding visible in the bin, and the contents will be brown and earthy looking worm castings. The contents will have substantially decreased in bulk.

It is important to separate the worms from the finished compost, otherwise the worms will begin to die. The quickest way to do this is to move the finished compost over to one side of the bin, place new bedding in the space created, and put food waste in the new bedding. The worms will gradually move over and the finished compost can be used as needed.

"If a healthy soil is full of death,
it is also full of life: worms, fungi,
microorganisms of all kinds...given
only the health of the soil, nothing
that dies is dead very long."

~Wendell Berry

....

chapter 3

Mulch

Mulch is needed on the surface of the soil to suppress weeds. Ir helps the soil to retain moisture and keep an even temperature.

It protects plants against wind, heavy rain and climate extremes.

It encourages worms so valuable in the aeration of the soil.

Organic mulches rot down and eventually provide nourishment for the soil.

They should be applied in loose, light 3-4 inch (8-10cm) layers so that air and water can reach the soil beneath.

INORGANIC MULCHES

Black plastic, tarred paper and aluminum foil will suppress weeds, prevent evaporation and warm the soil but they don't do much for the appearance of the garden

Mulching Tips

- A mulch should be between 2 to 4 inches thick for maximum benefits.

- Coarse mulch will stop weeds better, while a fine mulch will decompose easier, creating a need for more frequent mulching.

- Before mulching, remove weeds and soak the soil.

- Never mix mulch in with the soil. only place it on top.

when new, and look even worse as they become tatty.

But if you have weedy, unproductive pieces of ground, a cover of black plastic, weighed down with stones and left for some months will provide a weed-free and friable soil without any further effort.

Black plastic is widely used, and quite successfully, as a mulch for strawberry beds. It keeps the soil warm and moist, which is what the fruit likes, but in hot weather you have to keep an eye on the degree of heat generated.

Little pebbles and gravel make a decorative mulch, but don't do much more than trap heat and moisture, and can be the very devil to get rid of when you wish to make a change.

MATERIALS FOR ORGANIC MULCH

Leaves

Many people sweep up their fallen leaves and bag them ready for use.

A pile of leaves, lightly watered and left to rot will turn into a mold rich in nitrogen, potassium, phosphorus, magnesium and calcium in a reasonably short space of time. Mixed with grass clippings to keep the structure light, they make a wonderful mulch.

Fresh green leaves are best shredded and mixed with some grass clippings and a little soil which will prevent them from blowing away. An electric shredder is a boon and is the one thing an organic gardener cannot be without. You can keep running over leaves with a mower to break them up, but it is tedious.

It is unwise to put a pile of whole leaves down as mulch as they will turn into a solid mat, which will cut off air and water to the soil beneath.

Lawn Clippings

Never use mown grass fresh as the ammonia in it could burn plants. It is a good source of both nitrogen and potassium and best used mixed with other ingredients.

Garden Waste

Weeds, spent flowers and other green garden refuse are best chopped and left to wilt before being used as mulch. It is good mixed with small twigs and branches that have been put through the shredder. This gives a good C:N ratio.

Animal Manure

It must be well rotted to make sure it will not burn plants

- A thick layer of newspapers makes a good mulch, and since moset inks are vegetable based, they are nontoxic.

-Don't let mulch touch the stems of your plants. Only much to the "drip line" outside of plants.

or offend by its smell and is best used mixed with
other components. It is not recommended as a
mulch on its own but is valuable dried or in pellet
form mixed with other mulch materials to speed
their decomposition.

Stable manure is the least smelly. Chicken
manure, the most.

If you come by any fresh manure, mix it with sawdust and leave it in a heap,
out of sight, to decompose. You can pay the occasional visit to turn it over to let
air into it.

Newspaper

The ink used is no longer toxic, so newspaper is valuable both because it
will eventually rot down and nourish the soil (after all it comes from trees) and
because it will help to keep moisture in the soil. It doesn't look pretty used alone,
but screwed into loose balls and used under pine bark, wood chips, hay or straw
it is of use. Junk mail is no use—the inks are too highly colored and toxic, but old
envelopes, personal letters and bills can all be shredded and used.

Lucerne Hay

It pays to buy hay by the bale
whenever you can get hold of it. It stores
well. "Spoiled" hay, which just means
it is no longer suitable as animal feed—
usually because it has gotten wet and
become mildewy—is cheaper but just
fine for the garden.

Shake any seeds out of it and fluff it up before putting it down as mulch. Don't make the layers too deep, 1-1½ inches (3-4cm) will do.

It will decompose and release its nutrients gradually, and this suits plants very well. If you add leaves to it, decomposition will be delayed.

The light texture of fluffed-up hay allows air and water to reach the plants, but is strong enough to break up wind and give protection against hot sun.

Lucerne is said to give plants protection against diseases like root-rot and other fungal problems.

Straw

Straw doesn't have much to offer as a food for plants, but you can help it to rot more quickly by scattering pellets of chicken manure, blood, and bone over it. It isn't the prettiest mulch in the world.

Of course if you get stable straw, it will be enriched by the animal droppings. Don't use while the manure in it is still fresh.

Seaweed

This makes an excellent mulch as it is not only rich in potash but also contains trace elements. If you live near a beach, you will probably find the flat brown straps of kelp and bladder wrack strewn over the sand or clinging to the rocks after the tide has gone out.

If there is a tap at the beach, rinse it off to get rid of salt before bringing it home. You can use it chopped, on its own or mixed with other mulch ingredients.

Kelp

You can buy dehydrated seaweed and liquid seaweed extract. Use according to the manufacturer's instructions.

Mushroom Compost

Spent compost can be bought at most garden centers. It's very much the luck of the draw as to how much chemical fertilizer the grower has used but I have never heard anybody complain.

You can use it on its own. Mixed with grass clippings, it makes an excellent mulch for green vegetables.

The compost is usually made from a mix of chopped bracken or straw, peat moss and horse manure with an added trace of lime.

Bracken

Shred it, chop it, run over it with the mower—use it alone or mixed with other mulch ingredients; bracken makes a potassium rich mulch and is particularly good for potatoes. The ubiquitous ferns in the garden will not be so annoying once their worth is appreciated.

Sawdust

Good if used sparingly around plants to deter slugs and snails, but it is not recommended as a mulch in the garden bed for it is very acid.

You can get away with careful use if you only use old sawdust, mix it with a liberal helping of blood and bone meal and then add other mulch ingredients.

Always check to see if it has been made from timber treated with chemicals before you commit yourself to buying any.

The C:N ratio is 400:1 so you can imagine

how long it takes for it to break down to the 12:1 plants need it to be if they are to use it as good.

Wood Chips

You'll get a little more food value from wood chips but not a lot. Their best value is the cosmetic one. They look good in flower-beds and last a long time giving protection to the soil and preserving moisture, but they are not recommended for use in the vegetable garden because of their C:N ratio which is very little lower than sawdust.

Pine Bark and Pine Needles

Pine bark makes a dense and decorative mulch, particularly good for keeping weeds down and well-tolerated by acid-loving plants like azaleas, camellias and rhododendrons.

Strawberries grow well if surrounded by a mulch of pine needles 2-3 inches (7-8cm) deep. They like an acid soil with a pH around 5 to 6. Strawberries are usually in the ground for 3 years, so it will be necessary to replenish the mulch as it sinks in order to keep up the beneficial effect. Strawberries hate a waterlogged condition, so though the mulch should be kept moist, make certain drainage is adequate.

Pine bark takes a long time to decompose and will take nitrogen from the soil to help it to do so. You

Why Mulch Your Garden?

Apply to your vegetable garden in the second week of Spring each year:
1. Imitates the nutrient-saving nature of the forests.
2. Eliminates water splash and the soil-borne diseases.
3. Suppresses weeds.
4. Controls nutrient loss through leaching in heavy rain.
5. Prevents the soil getting a hard crust.
6. Encourages wormlife to work at the soil surface accelerating soil improvement.
7. Adds humus creating organic matter to the top of the soil.

can replace this by scattering some blood and bone meal or dried chicken manure under the bark.

Comfrey

Comfrey

Regarded by herbalists and organic gardeners alike as a wonder plant, comfrey proves its worth by the many uses to which it can be put. Rich in potassium, nitrogen, phosphates, calcium and vitamin B12, it makes a splendid plant food when used as a mulch. Chopped and well-soaked, it can go directly on to the soil. If you have a spare piece of ground, you will not regret planting it up with comfrey. It takes too long to grow from seed, so most people either buy young plants from a nursery or cadge sections of root that show a bud from any friend or neighbor with it in their garden. These root cuttings usually take easily and grow quickly and strongly.

Comfrey likes a moist and shady spot but is not fussy about the quality of the topsoil as its roots go deep in search of nourishment. It makes a tall, hearty plant with big hairy leaves and white flower spikes. Go for as many plants as you can possibly accommodate—you will find use for them all.

Besides making good compost, it is a compost invigorator and can be used to make liquid manure.

Feathers

If you have old pillows or an old eiderdown—and you are game—you can use the feathers, which are high in nitrogen as mulch. They will have to be soaked, chopped and left to rot in an out-of-the-way spot for some time until they can be incorporated into a mixed mulch.

Wood Ash

Use mixed with other mulch material and keep it from touching plants. Store dry—if it gets wet, the potash will leak away.

Peat Moss

This is a bit tricky to use. If you don't keep it moist enough it will suck up what it needs from the soil. If you let it get too dry, it will blow away and, since it is not cheap, that can be irritating. It is best used in conjunction with other mulch materials.

Gathering materials for use as mulch and compost is a constant preoccupation. Some material will be used at once, others will have to be stored. Green and dried waste can be safely left piled in the open; food scraps go into a sealed bucket—but only for a short time.

"By the deficiency or absence of one necessary constituent, all the others being present, the soil is rendered barren for all those crops to the life of which that one constituent is indispensable."

Julius Von Liebig,
German physical soil chemist, 1840

. . . .

chapter 4

Fertilizers for the Soil

The fertility of the soil is an organic gardener's preoccupation and its enrichment, without the use of chemical fertilizers, a constant task.

The best all-round fertilizer is compost, which contains so much valuable organic matter. But it is not always the perfect answer. If compost is only made from materials grown on impoverished soil, it will be as lacking in nutrients as the soil from which they came. So it is important to make as wide a mix as possible of materials that contain as many as possible of the elements soil needs for maximum health. A cake can only be as good as the ingredients!

Along with compost, manure is vital to the health of the soil. Happiness is access to henhouse, byre and stable.

ANIMAL MANURE

Along with compost, manure is vital to the health of the soil. Happiness is access to henhouse, byre and stable.

Horse Manure

Race-horse owners and breeders have recourse to hormone treatment and antibiotics, so refuse from their stables is no use to the organic gardener, but local owners who just keep a horse for the joy of it are worth cultivating as friends and could be as grateful for your offer to "muck out" as you will be for the booty you carry away.

Lucerne hay or oat straw, saturated in urine is gardener's gold. Horse-owners are usually horse-lovers and feed their animal on more than grass, so the nutritional value of the droppings can be high. Horse manure is higher in nitrogen than that of cow, pig, sheep, goat and rabbit and is what is called a "hot" manure because it will burn the roots and stems of plants with which it comes into contact. It cannot be used fresh.

It should be added to the compost heap where it will help the contents to break down more quickly—not too much at a time.

If you have enough to store, cover it tightly to keep out the rain and to prevent the escape of nitrogen. A thick layer of soil or sawdust is sometimes used, but black plastic does the job well too.

Horse manure should not be dug into the soil but shredded and spread over the surface and left for soil organisms to work on.

Cow Manure

Since it is fairly low in nitrogen it is not a "hot" manure, it can be used safely directly on to the soil almost as soon as it has stopped steaming.

It makes a useful addition to the compost heap.

Old and well-rotted, it makes a good addition to a "sheet" compost. It retains water well and makes an excellent mulch. Break up and shred dry pats before use.

Sheep Manure

Most of the sheep manure comes from the mass of droppings that have piled up under shearing sheds. It contains more potassium than other animal manures. The hard pellets won't break down unless they are moistened, so wet the ground where they are needed, sprinkle with the amount of manure needed, wet it and then cover it with a good mixed mulch. The initial watering will give breakdown a boost and subsequent regular waterings will continue the process.

If you collect fresh pellets while walking in the country, add them to the compost heap. Goat and sheep manure are exchangeable.

Pig Manure

If you have a personal pig or know a friendly farmer who keeps one, you are in luck, for you will know what the animal has been fed on and can use the ordure without fear. Professional pig breeders are known to have recourse to hormones,

antibiotics, etc. to promote size and fat content, so heaven knows what is excreted in the pig waste.

Since this is a "cold" manure and takes a long time to break down, it is best used as an addition to the compost heap.

Poultry and Bird Manures

Chicken manure though far too "hot" to be used fresh can be the backbone of an organic garden.

It can be used mixed with old leaves, straw, chopped weeds and lawn mowings as a mulch provided it does not touch the stems or roots of plants. But is far better used old and dried.

If you have enough to store, cover it well to protect it from the rain and to prevent the escape of nitrogen. Some people make a thick soil covering. Black plastic, securely weighted down does well too.

Leave until the pile is thoroughly dry and is no longer smelly. Well-decayed, this is **the** soil fertilizer. It has a good NPK and contains important trace elements. It makes a good compost activator.

Deep litter from the henhouse, impregnated with urine and droppings, is a good provider of humus, but the droppings by themselves are not. The NPK of the litter is twice that of droppings used alone.

Pigeon Manure

If you know a pigeon fancier, do yourself a good turn by offering to clean out the cages in return for being allowed to keep the mess.

Pigeon manure is higher in food value than chicken manure and just as likely to burn plants if used fresh. Store droppings for about a month, well-covered.

When dried the droppings can be carefully pulverized and used as a side-dressing for all members of the brassica family.

Dried manures are, of course, obtainable from nurseries and garden shops. Whatever did we do before the day of the dried chicken pellet?

A browse among the organic fertilizers now on sale will provide much valuable information.

I have found considerable discrepancy in the NPK tables supplied by experts and since the home gardener has no way of proving things to personal satisfaction, take them as a rough guide.

Feathers, human hair, hoof and horn meal are all very much richer in nitrogen than any of the animal manures.

I have yet to find two experts who agree on the exact percentages. One estimate goes as follows:

Horse and cow 6% to 7%

Bone meal 6%

Hoof and horn meal, 12.5%

Hair 14%

Feathers 15%

The difference is marked. The good thing about the highly-concentrated material is that nitrogen is released slowly at a rate compatible with a plant's ability to cope with it.

Feathers and human hair should be chopped and kept moist to enable decomposition to get under way.

Hair that has been dyed or otherwise treated with chemicals is not suitable for use.

Blood and Bone Meal

This is probably the most often bought organic fertilizer. It is clean to handle and easy to distribute.

The blood content supplies nitrogen; the bone content, phosphorus and calcium—it is not a complete fertilizer as it is short on potassium. The addition of wood-ash, or a 10% admixture of sulfate of potash puts that right.

The meal breaks down slowly and the nutrients are released over a period of time—this suits both the growing plants and the denizens of the soil. Warmth and moisture will speed decomposition. The meal can be used directly on the soil, or added to the compost heap and mulch to give them extra nutritional quality and to speed up breakdown of the constituents.

Seaweed

Seaweed is not a fertilizer but it improves the texture of the soil so well that

A GUIDE TO NPK FOR ANIMAL MANURE

	Nitrogen	Phosphorus	Potassium
Hen	1.1 to 2.1	0.8 to 1.6	0.5 to 1.0
Sheep	0.7 to 1.8	0.3 to 0.4	0.9 to 0.5
Pig	0.5 to 1.0	0.3 to 0.7	0.5 to 0.1
Cow	0.6 to 1.0	0.2 to 0.4	0.5
Horse	0.7	0.3	0.6
Pig	0.5 to 1.0	0.3 to 0.7	0.5 to 0.1

It is important to keep the correct acid/alkaline balance of the soil as shortages of calcium, copper, zinc, and molybdenum show up on acid soil and shortages of iron, manganese and boron on alkaline soils.

it enables the inhabitants to do a better job. If you are able to collect any from a beach after high tide or a storm, it is advisable to hose it down before bringing it home. I used to think it was to remove excess salt, but seaweed actually contains very little salt. I still hose it down though, to clean debris off and to minimize the smell.

Seaweed should not be dug into the ground, but used, chopped, in a mulch (see what I mean about the smell) or added to the compost bin. Fortunately it decomposes quite quickly. It makes a particularly good mulch for asparagus.

If you were to dig it into the ground, the bacteria and soil organisms would have to pinch nitrogen from the soil to enable them to start breaking it down and you would be faced with a nitrogen shortage.

Dried seaweed and seaweed emulsions are on sale at most garden shops.

Well diluted with water, the emulsion can be used as a spray to encourage the breakdown of mulch materials. Since it contains trace elements and potassium, it is a better moistening agent than just water.

See FOLIAR FEEDING

THE NUTRIENTS PLANTS NEED TO FIND IN THE SOIL

Nitrogen for leaf growth

Phosphorus for root growth

Potassium (potash) to aid digestion

Calcium for the building of strong cell walls
Magnesium to encourage chlorophyll production
Sulphur to encourage chlorophyll production
Iron to assist in the formation of chlorophyll
Zinc and copper as enzyme activators
Manganese to assist in the formation of
chlorophyll and proteins
Molybdeum to prevent distortion in growth
Boron to encourage tissue growth

Nitrogen

Nitrogen is necessary for leaf growth. The nitrates, so valuable in the process of photosynthesis, are soluble and seep away with the soil water.

The dictionary definition of photosynthesis is "the synthesis of carbohydrates by plants from carbon dioxide and water, using sunlight, absorbed by chlorophyll and other pigments as a source of energy."

Nitrogen is a major component of chlorophyll, so without an adequate supply of it, the complicated process can break down. Obviously care must be taken to keep up the supply and, as far as possible, to prevent nitrates leaching away. "Fixing" nitrogen in the soil is not difficult. Rhizobium bacteria in the soil and the roots of plants like pea, bean, clover, lupin and lucerne, act on one another to "fix" it. The home garden is seldom large enough to grow a crop of one of them especially for the purpose, so it is important to keep the soil covered with a nitrogen-rich mulch and to top it up as the lower layer breaks down.

Green leaves and stems, seaweed, hay, fowl manure, feathers, urine, blood and bone meal, grass mowings are all rich in nitrogen.

Signs of deficiency

The plants are weak and stunted; leaves limp and yellow.

Phosphorus

Phosphorus does not leach out of the soil, but if the soil is too acid or too alkaline it keeps the phosphorus insoluble and so quite useless as plant food. To help release it, add compost to the soil, correct the pH balance and keep up a good mulch so that there are plenty of soil organisms at work. Blood and bone meal, chicken, and pig droppings, lobster and eggshells all contain phosphorus.

Ground phosphate rock—not the super-phosphate widely used by farmers—scattered over the soil will help. One application should last four or five years so don't buy a lot.

Signs of deficiency

Look for poor root development with stunted growth and bad-looking leaves.

Quick Source Reference

Nitrogen:
Green leaves and stems. Fowl Manure. Blood and bone meal. Feathers. Urine. Hay. Seaweed. Grass mowings.

Phosphorus:
Blood and bone meal. Chicken, pigeon and pig manure. Egg shells. Lobster shells. Ground phosphate rock.

Potassium:
Green leaves and twigs. Seaweed. Wood ash. Bone meal. Comfrey. Animal manure.

Potassium

The supply must be steady as it is needed to help plants to digest food, and it leaches away easily.

If the soil is too acid, it becomes insoluble and of no food value.

Seaweed, wood ash, green leaves and twigs, animal manure, comfrey and bonemeal are all good sources of supply. Permanganate of potash, chamomile, nettle, dandelion all contain some too.

Correct the pH balance and make sure there is plenty of organic material in the soil and you should have enough potassium.

Signs of deficiency

Weak stems. Limp leaves

From the signs of deficiency, it can be seen that the exact shortage can be very hard to detect. Nitrogen could be the most likely. If you correct that and make sure the soil is adequately fed and kept as near a neutral pH as possible and plants are still not thriving, you should be able to pinpoint the trouble.

OTHER ELEMENTS PLANTS NEED

Calcium

Needed to make strong cell walls, calcium is found in lime, dolomite and wood ash. Chives, chamomile, dandelion, nettle, comfrey, horsetail.

Signs of deficiency

Tips of new shoots wilt, leaves curl and become discolored. The soil is too acid.

Magnesium

Magnesium is needed to keep up the supply of chlorophyll. It is found in dolomite and Epsom salts, dandelion, parsley.

Signs of deficiency

Older leaves turn yellow and fall.

Sulphur

Sulfur is needed for the formation of chlorophyll. It is found in nettles and other organic substances.

Signs of deficiency

Stunted, yellowing leaves. Trace elements needed.

Manganese

Needed for the formation of proteins and chlorophyll. It is found in compost, wood ash, sawdust, horse manure, permanganate of potash, dandelion.

Signs of deficiency

Young leaves turn yellow.

Copper and Zinc

Needed as enzyme activators. Copper is found in nettles and yarrow. Zinc is found in cornstalks.

Signs of deficiency

Leaves become mottled and yellow. The deficiency occurs most frequently in acid, sandy soils.

Boron

Boron is needed to regulate the plant's use of nitrogen. It is found in horse manure, sawdust, compost and wood ash.

Signs of deficiency

Stems become hollow and break, buds rot, citrus fruit becomes brown and soggy in the center. The deficiency occurs most frequently when soil is alkaline.

Molybdenum

Needed to prevent growth deformities. It is found in horse manure, sawdust, compost and wood ash, horsetail and corn stalks.

Signs of deficiency

New growth is distorted. "Whiptail" in brassica is a sure sign. The deficiency occurs most frequently in soil that is too acid.

Kitchen Waste Fertilizer

If you have a largish garden you could bury kitchen waste just as it is, but you will have to make sure the holes you dig are deep enough to ensure everything is out of reach of enterprising vermin. Sixteen inches (40cm) deep and just as wide is the least you can expect to get away with.

Choose an unused part of the garden that you would like to bring up to scratch and dig your first hole. Half fill it with waste.

Dig another hole the same size close to the first one, and throw the soil over the waste as you go until the first hole is filled up and the waste well covered.

Any soil left over can be piled ready to add as the waste sinks. Continue making holes and filling them up as needed until you have used up all the ground you want to fertilize.

It will take six to eight months for the waste to rot but it won't require any attention during that time.

Don't plant anything in the soil above the waste until you are absolutely certain it has all rotted down, otherwise there could be risk of infection.

Chemical Fertilizers

You might think that an element, like potash, is a food plants need so why worry if you give it to them in chemical form—they've got it, haven't they? The answer is, not really. They have trouble digesting it: it isn't in a form they can readily absorb.

This is true of all chemical fertilizers. No chemical fertilizer can produce humus, not a smidgin of it, and humus is the life of the soil and the food nature provides for her plants.

Worms, bacteria and other organisms in the soil work on organic matter and turn it into a simple and easily assimilated food.

In nature, the cycle is continuous—things grow and die, return to the earth, are assimilated and give life to the soil so that a new generation of plants can be nourished. It is presumptuous to think we can improve on the process.

The mistake that has been made in the past has been to think of the plant as requiring food and assiduously feeding what we thought was needed while completely neglecting the needs of the soil. It's a case of first things first: feed the soil, for then the plant will get what it needs in the form that it likes and can easily digest.

Green Manuring

You need a large garden if you are to go in for green manuring. This is the practice of sowing a crop for the sole purpose of cutting it down and incorporating it into the soil to improve it. If you have a problem area over-run by recalcitrant weeds or your soil is too sandy or too clayey it is worth a go on a small scale. The object of the exercise is to get humus into the soil to aerate and enrich it as quickly as possible so the obvious choice is for leafy, fast-growing crops. The choice is wide.

The Leguminosae Family

The leguminosae family, which does such a good job of fixing nitrogen in the soil, is an obvious one. Have a go with broad beans or peas. There is no need to be fussy about the way you sow, thick and indiscriminate will do but if the soil in which you sow them is poor, feed it—there is no point in raising a sickly crop. Blood and bone, compost—your own good stuff—or bought mushroom compost and a flick of lime won't go amiss. Cut down when the plants are flowering, don't wait longer than that. You can either dig it in but only shallowly, or leave it to rot on the top of the soil for the worms to have a go at it. Chop it up to make easy feeding for them and water it gently. A bit of blood and bone will accelerate decomposition.

Mustard

Mustard is another quick-growing crop but has disadvantages in that it attracts white butterflies, which do damage to brassica crops and are subject to the same diseases as they are.

Rye, Buckwheat, Oats, Sunflowers

Rye, buckwheat, oats and sunflowers are also worth consideration—they draw nutrients from deep within the soil. So is clover, which is a good nitrogen fixer. Radish, grown between other crops but left to die, will also enrich the soil.

Marigolds

Nematodes hate marigolds, which can be ornamental as well as useful. I'm not certain if they should be dug in before they flower but I let mine have their head before cutting them down just for the pleasure of seeing them and because I feel you can never go wrong with marigolds.

Brambles and Lantana

Brambles and lantana can be hell to get rid of—all you can do is to dig as much of them out as you can and inhibit any further growth by trying to smother them with quick-growing "green manure."

Rye

LIQUID MANURING

Liquid manure is not a substitute for fresh or dried manure and should not be regarded as a soil-enriching agent. Plants make quick use of the food it offers and, since it is in liquid form, anything left will easily leach away.

It should be regarded as a quick feed, delivered to plants when and where they want it—a plant rescue remedy. Its other good use is as a boost to the breakdown of organic materials in compost and mulch.

Liquid fertilizer made from plants is used as a foliar feed.

Animal Manures

Some manures are "hotter" than others so don't mix them. A separate brew of cow and chicken manure is best.

You can make a small supply in a bucket.

Three quarters fill the bucket with water. Balance a piece of strong wood such as a broom handle cut to size across it.

Fill the foot-end of a pair of pantyhose with manure, fresh or dried. Knot just above it, then cut off a length of leg long enough to tie around the broom handle to allow the manure to dangle in the water.

When the water becomes straw-colored, you can use it on the soil, but be careful not to let any of it spill on the stem or leaves of the plant.

If you let it stand for a few days—covered with a large old piece of cloth to keep the flies away—the water will have become dark brown. Dilute it until the color of straw before using.

If you want a large and constant supply you will need large containers, lidded for preference. If they don't have lids, you will have to improvise and find something suitable.

A lid is very important, not only because without it nitrogen could be lost to the air, but because the smell will attract flies and the open water will bring mosquitoes.

You can either two-thirds fill the bin with water and then scoop your manure into it or use the dangle method with the manure in an old pillowcase or sack.

You could have a visit to the bin every few days to give it a stir or to dunk the bag up and down a few times. You have to lean over the bin to give the contents a good stir, so take a deep breath or put a handkerchief over your nose!

There seems to be two schools of thought about how to go about things. One says put the lid on firmly and go away and forget it for a month. The other says visit it daily, give it a dunk or stir, skim off the scum and add it to the compost heap and, after two weeks start using the liquid, always putting back as much water as you take out.

I can't see that it matters how you go about things provided you always dilute the liquid manure until it becomes a pale yellow before you use it.

Making Liquid Manure

To make your own liquid manure all you need is a large container to hold water, a hessian bag and some animal manure. Some plants, such as comfrey, can also be used. Most animal manures can be used but sheep manure is particularly high in nutrients. You should water the soil before using your home-made liquid manure. To use a foliar spray the liquid should be diluted with equal parts of water.

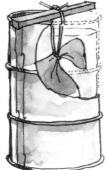

1. Fill a drum with water and collect a bag of animal droppings. Tie the top to create a loop at the top.

2. Put a piece of wood across the top of the container and suspend the bag in the water. Leave the bag for about 2 weeks. The water will go dark brown. Remove the bag and cover.

WARNING:

Don't be tempted to think that a strong brew will do more good than a weaker one—it won't. It will either burn the plant or give it such a bad dose of indigestion that it will wilt.

Those plastic containers with a handle and a lid used to present honey for sale make useful little "buckets" for scooping out liquid for immediate use.

The liquid from cow manure has to be one part of liquid to 10 parts of water. Check the color. Hen manure is stronger stuff and needs 20 to 25 parts of water to one of liquid. Always use your common sense and go by the color.

The liquid should be poured, carefully and slowly on to the soil around the plants. The dose can be repeated every fortnight during the growing season.

Weeds

Deep-rooting weeds can bring up nutrients from the sub-soil. Others contain chlorophyll, iron, etc. Why not make a "tea" from them as an alternative to throwing them into the compost heap. Chop up weeds, and leave soaking well covered with water in a container. After three weeks you will have a green tea, which can be poured on to the soil around plants. The sludge can go into your mulch or compost heap.

Nettles

Nettles contain chlorophyll, protein, iron, silica, sulfur, potassium, sodium and some of the vitamins A, B and C so it makes good sense to use them to make a liquid fertilizer.

Gather as many nettles as you can, put them in a container commensurate in size with the amount you were able to collect, cover them with water and give them a good press and stir, then cover the pot or bin securely and leave to ferment for about 3 weeks. The nettles will now be sludge at the bottom of the container and the water richly colored.

Dilute the water until the color of weak tea or pale sherry before using as a plant food. It makes a good spring tonic.

If you use it as a foliar feed, strain it through a pair of old pantyhose first to prevent it blocking the spray.

If you have only a few nettles, don't waste them—make the plants a pot of tea and let it stand until cold before you give it to them.

The sludge makes a good addition to mulch and compost.

Dandelions

The dandelion contains iron, copper, protein, fat, insulin, potassium, manganese and calcium besides a range of vitamins. Since I don't know which part of the plant contains what, I use the whole plant when I can, and just the leaves and stems when I can't.

Dig the plants up, chop them and leave to soak in water, covered for two or

three weeks. Dilute the water until the color of weak tea or pale sherry and use to water the soil around plants or as a foliar feed.

Try and pinch other people's dandelions and leave the ones in your own garden where they are. They give off an ethylene gas that encourages plants in the vicinity to mature and ripen.

Comfrey

Comfrey contains nitrogen, phosphorus and potassium, all elements plants need as food and has a reputation for good that runs clear down the centuries. It is a big plant and the leaves are big and coarse. Collect as many as you can from wherever you can find them—best of all grow your own, as many plants as you can for you will find use for all of them, either as mulch or for making liquid manure.

Half fill a container with leaves, fill it up with water, cover it and leave for about 3 weeks with the occasional visit for the purpose of giving it a good stir. You can then ladle water out for use and put an equal amount of clean water in as recompense. The leaves contain a lot of water so they rot down quite easily. Any slush left can be added to mulch or compost.

The "tea" should be diluted until the color of pale sherry before giving to the plants.

Since comfrey contains calcium and vitamin B12, you could try it as tea made in a pot, and served with a slice of lemon and honey to taste. For you, not for the plants. For a pot that contains about half a liter, use 3 or 4 leaves, washed and cut up.

"And so it criticized each flower, This supercilious seed; Until it woke one summer hour, And found itself a weed."

~Mildred Howells

. . . .

chapter 5

Weeds

You don't see many weeds in an organic garden—they are mostly buried under mulch—and those that are there by invitation.

"Weed" is such an accusing and derogatory word, but once you start to think of them as plants that just happen to be where you don't want them to be you see them in a different light. It is difficult to develop an affection for the weeds that reappear so persistently in the cracks between the paving or the oxalis whose tiny bulbs are so maddeningly intractable, but I never mind finding chickweed in the lawns. It comes out so easily, is so succulent and rich in iron and copper that it makes a splendid addition to the compost heap. Other annual weeds spell nitrogen more than nuisance as they too are fed to the heap.

Dandelions are more than welcome—this plant is one of the richest in the whole plant kingdom. It contains iron, copper, protein and a range of vitamins and minerals. When the plant has produced its first flowers, cut off the stems and leaves and add them to the compost and leave the root to push up more growth for you.

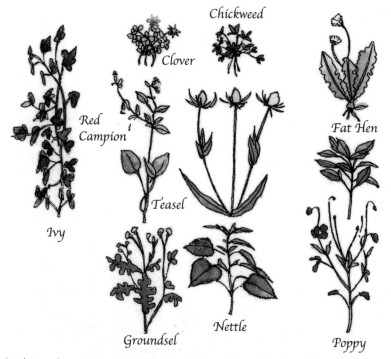

Weeds can be put to use in the organic garden with exception of those with ripe seed heads or bulbous roots. Pull or slash weeds regularly to prevent them from setting seed and spreading.

Destroy Weeds with Mulch

If you have a new patch of ground that you want to break in and plant up but which is covered with weeds and which, to the conventional gardener, would spell hours of digging, turning soil over and searching for weed roots, take the easy way instead. Cover the soil with black plastic, peg it or weigh it down round the edges and leave it for as long as you can for the weeds and their roots to be smothered and die. This is the  patient way. If you can't wait, cover the soil with a deep mulch—a really deep one—and plant in that. You will have to give each seedling a little pocket of compost in which to establish roots. The expensive way is to use bought plastic weed mats that you plant through. Tricky to plant out and worrisome with regard to food and water I have found, but friends use them happily and they are worth a try.

The main thing is not to pull the weeds out but to cover them up and encourage them to die and enrich the soil.

Covering the soil with mulch prevents weed seeds from germinating but deep-rooted weeds are harder to eliminate. I don't mind even them all that much. If they have the strength to push up through the mulch, think of all the nutrients they have brought up from way down below and are there in the leaves. Cutting them off and adding to the compost and leaving them to try again seems sensible.

If you mulch well, weeds are not that much of a problem, some are a great deal more persistent than others—couch grass for example. But even that old enemy is weakened by the use of mulch for the roots cannot get as firm a hold as they would like and the grass is easy to pull out. Try pouring neat urine that has been allowed to stand for 3 days over it—and only it—not the surrounding plants. This usually kills it off.

Couch roots and bulblets of oxalis and onion grass should not be fed to the compost when you pull them out. Chuck them in a bucket of water and leave to rot for a week or two first.

If the situation is desperate, you could torch the weeds—or weather and law permitting—build a wide spread of garden rubbish and set fire to it. You will then have to work on the baked earth on which the bonfire stood to loosen and enrich it again before being able to use it.

Weeds invade a conventional garden because there is so much bare soil in it—in the organic garden there is practically no bare soil and so no welcome for them. You can never expect to be without weeds entirely, but would you really want to be? They are friends as well.

"The secret to good, friable soil with high humus, good aeration and water retaining properties is a simple matter of adding organic material, and allowing the worms to do the work."

~Paul Healy

chapter 6

Garden Beds

Few of us have the luxury of planning a garden from scratch. Most of us have to deal with what we have inherited and are faced by the choices made by other people whose tastes and lifestyle may be very far from our own. Tastes and needs differ so widely that it seems presumptuous to tell anybody what to do with their garden, but, whether you are making glorious plans for your new pristine plot or are prowling around wondering what on earth you are going to do to knock this lot into shape, there are few basic questions to be answered. Time spent walking the boundaries and looking around with narrowed eyes and an active imagination at work is never wasted. Most people require their garden to supply them with

a place for the grown-ups to sit out, a place for the children to play and room to grow flowers, veggies, fruit and herbs.

An inspection of the garden will show which areas have the most shade, the most sun, where the good soil is and where the damp lies.

A SPOT FOR THE VEGETABLES

Is the spot chosen handy for the taps or will you have to put more in?

Is there a shed near where you can store garden tools and mowers or will you have to traipse back to the garage each time you need them?Is there room for a compost heap or bin, or both? Is there a room for storing the materials to be made into compost and into mulch?

Do you want any of these features to be visible from the house windows?

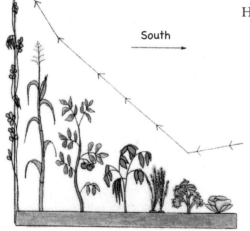

South

Have you enough room to plant all you need? If you haven't, what about using some, if not all of the lawn? It is the easiest thing in the world to turn an expanse of grass into a garden bed; no heavy digging is involved, you just build the bed on top of it. You can probably think of many more questions to ask. Another that springs to mind is, do I want a shade house or a cold frame? The important thing is to ask them all sooner rather than later.

Maximizing sun angles and deflecting hot winds with a rising foliage slope.

The convention of keeping flowers, vegetables and herbs confined to their own places in the garden is no longer the hard and fast rule. They can grow very happily, and often, very prettily together and do each other a power of good too.

See COMPANION PLANTING.

When planning a vegetable bed leave space for a border of flowers or herbs round it.

It is nice to have herbs growing near to the kitchen—the easier they are to reach the more you will use them. If you don't have space for a plot at least make room near the back door for some big pots.

You'll be very lucky if you get your planning right the first time—so often a garden plan evolves of itself—you live it into existence, so to speak. And why not? A garden reflects the personality, taste and lifestyle of its owner and much of its charm lies in that unmistakable individuality.

BUILDING A GARDEN BED

Establishing a garden bed the traditional way can be hard and heavy work, particularly if the soil is poor and requires double-digging and the inclusion of fertilizers.

The organic gardener's way of dealing with soil that is over-run with weeds, or worn out, or heavy

Double Digging

Double digging can improve a vegetable garden by incorporating air and organic material deep into the root zones.

1. Using a spade, make a trench 1 ft. (30 cm) wide and one spade deep. Put the soil in a pile at the edge of the trench.

2. Loosen the soil in the bottom of the trench.

3. Next fill the trench half way with compost.

4. Dig a second trench adjacent to the first and place the soil on top of the compost you placed in the first trench. Mix the soil and compost together with the spade.

5. Fill the last trench with the soil you removed from the first.

with clay, or light and gritty with sand, is to build a new garden bed over the top
of it. The work isn't heavy because the organic materials used are light and easy
to handle and there is an added bonus—before too long the soil that has been
covered will have become healthy and friable due to the action of the organisms
contained in the organic matter which, after dealing with the top layers, will

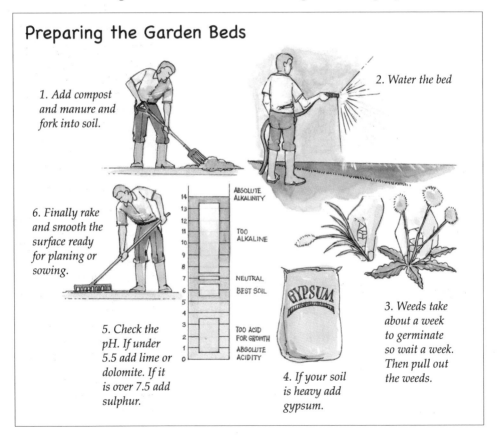

Preparing the Garden Beds

1. Add compost and manure and fork into soil.

2. Water the bed

6. Finally rake and smooth the surface ready for planing or sowing.

14 — ABSOLUTE ALKALINITY
13
12
11 — TOO ALKALINE
10
9
8
7 — NEUTRAL
6 — BEST SOIL
5
4
3 — TOO ACID FOR GROWTH
2
1 — ABSOLUTE ACIDITY
0

5. Check the pH. If under 5.5 add lime or dolomite. If it is over 7.5 add sulphur.

GYPSUM

4. If your soil is heavy add gypsum.

3. Weeds take about a week to germinate so wait a week. Then pull out the weeds.

work their way downwards, opening up compacted soil so that air and moisture, organic matter and other soil organisms can find their way into it.

Because no preparation of the soil is needed this way of doing things has been dubbed the NO-DIG method.

Choose your spot and define the area of the bed. The width should allow you to reach the middle from either side, the length is up to you. It is helpful to have a path running the entire length of the bed on either side.

Chop down annual weeds and use a weeding-fork to pull out the weeds of perennial ones. You could just mow the area, but you know how determined perennial weed roots can be.

Alternatively you could cut down everything growing in the patch, sprinkle well with a high nitrogenous fertilizer (blood and bone, dried chicken pellets, old manure, etc.) and then soak the ground before covering it with thick black plastic, firmly held down. This will have to stay in place for some weeks. Planks around the edges work best as they are easier to move than the number of large stones it would take to keep the plastic anchored.

If you don't want to wait, fertilize and wet the cleared ground and then cover it with overlapping sheets of newspaper—thick wads of it. Soak the wads.

Spread a 6-8-inch (15-20cm) layer of mixed loose coarse, organic material over the area—spoilt hay, straw, litter from the henhouse and horse-box, corn stalks, thin twigs, etc. Then add not-so-coarse materials, chopped green stuff, leaves, some green, some dead, seaweed, grass mowings, etc. Some old dried shredded manure—cow, horse and fowl, NOT pig. Cover with a thin layer of ordinary soil sprinkled with blood and bone meal and water.

The top layer should be of compost and about 4 inches (10cm) deep.

If you can manage to wait a week so much the better, but if you cannot go carefully. Shallow-rooted seedlings can be planted in the compost.

To accommodate longer-rooted ones, make a hole down through the compost into the layers of organic matter beneath, fill the hole with your own compost or some bought mushroom compost and plant the seedling, making sure the roots are not in contact with the decomposing materials.

From now on it is just a matter of adding mulch, regularly and continuously, so that organisms are always present and at work.

The mulch should be kept light and damp, never allowed to coagulate and cut off air and water to the material and soil beneath.

Keeping a bed like this at just the right degree of dampness is just about all the maintenance required.

TRENCH METHOD

If you live where the climate is mostly dry and hot, or even if you want to grow plants that require heavy watering, the trench method will suit you.

The advantages are that, growing in the trench, plants are protected against the hot sun and do not lose water from their leaves to the same extent as plants growing in the open. The soil is also protected against the sun and will not dry out as quickly.

Method

1. A narrow trench, one to three spades in depth, according to the height of the plants you wish to grow will be fine.

2. Break up the soil at the bottom of the trench, put down a layer of coarse materials,

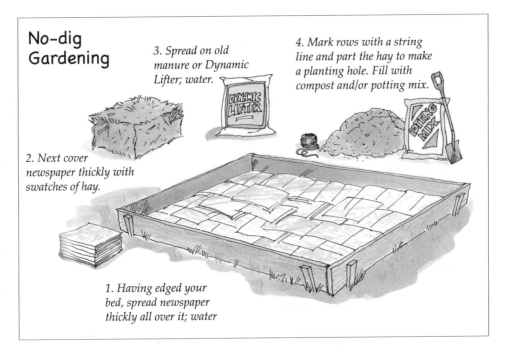

No-dig Gardening

3. Spread on old manure or Dynamic Lifter; water.

4. Mark rows with a string line and part the hay to make a planting hole. Fill with compost and/or potting mix.

2. Next cover newspaper thickly with swatches of hay.

1. Having edged your bed, spread newspaper thickly all over it; water

twigs, bracken, corn stalks, etc. and then cover that with hay.

3. Hay lifts off the bale in layers. Use a layer, fluffing it up just a bit. Add anything good you have on hand—chopped seaweed, comfrey, dandelion, etc.

4. Cover this with a layer of compost at least 4 inches (10cm) deep.

5. Turn the hose on and really soak the hay, etc. and leave for a short time to settle.

6. Plant out and keep mulching as the plants grow.

Since the initial watering has been so heavy and the trench gives insulation, frequent watering should not be a problem. When the top of the mulch starts to feel dry, leave the hose to trickle into the trench until the mulch feels damp, but is not soggy.

Keep a watchful eye to see that damp mulch is not touching the stems of young seedlings. When the stems strengthen and harden, it will not matter so much, but in their early stages they need protection against the dreaded damping-off.

SHEET COMPOSTING

Initially this requires you to get busy with spade.

After you've marked out the bed, turn the soil over to a depth of 6-8 inches (15-20cm), break up any lumps and rake to a fine tilth. Check to see what sort of soil it is.

If the reading on a soil testing kit reads a pH less than 5 or if litmus paper used to make the test turns blue, you have acid soil which needs sweetening. You can use wood ash, hydrated lime or dolomite. Dolomite is gentler and does not act as quickly as the lime.

If the reading is over 7, the soil is too alkaline and you will need to mix in some rotted leaves or peat, sawdust, etc.

When the pH balance is about 6.5, you can put down fertilizer. You will need about half a cupful of dried fertilizer for each 11 square feet (1 square meter).

Blood and bone meal needs an admixture of 10% sulfate of potash to make it into an all-round fertilizer. Mix the amount you need for the size of the bed before distributing it.

Now spread the bed with old well-rotted horse, sheep or cow manure—half a bucket to 11 square feet (1 square meter) and cover that with a layer of bought mushroom compost deep enough to conceal the manure.

Fork the additions into the soil—not deeply—6-8 inches (15-20cm) is enough.

Now water well and leave the bed to settle. From one weekend to the next will suit many gardeners. You can now sow or plant the bed.

Wait until the young plants are growing well and then spread the ground all round them with a mixture of organic material. NO KITCHEN OR FOOD SCRAPS. The leaves, weeds, dried leaves, dead flowers, flower and corn stalks, sawdust, newspaper, etc., should all be chopped and the mixture of "green" and "brown" waste made carefully to maintain a good C:N ratio.

From an aesthetic point of view this "sheet" could leave a lot to be desired but if you mix hay with it, the appearance will improve. If you don't mind the look of straw, you could use that too.

When the layer is down, sprinkle it generously with old, shredded manure or dried natural fertilizer. Finally, water the bed well.

As the plants grow and the "sheet" decomposes, add more and continue to do so, right through the growing season.

WARNING: ⚠

Do not allow damp mulch to touch seedlings, as damping off could occur.

Advantages and Drawbacks

The drawback of this method is the amount of spadework needed.

The advantage is that the attention given to the soil in the early stages gets seed or plants off to a good, quick start as they go straight into nutritious surroundings. By waiting until the young plants are growing well before putting the "sheet" down means that the sun has had a chance to warm the soil and so the plants have a further boost.

If you use both non-dig and the "sheet" method, you will notice how much longer it takes plants in the no-dig garden to get going. This is because the mulch has kept the ground cool and they also have to wait for the mulch to decay and turn into a good supply of food.

RAISED BEDS

A raised bed can look very attractive and the labor of creating it is soon forgotten in the pleasure it gives. If you have a problem spot in the garden—soil poor, shape awkward, a mecca for local dogs who regard it as a comfort station—a raised bed could solve all your problems. Once it is built it is so much easier to maintain than a bed at ground level and having more or less eye-to-eye contact with the plants, leads to a closer relationship between you and them.

Raised beds have several advantages over flat beds. The bed is narrow enough that you can work in it without walking in it, so the soil is never compacted. Raised beds drain better than flat beds, and they warm up faster in spring.

Beds can have no sides at all if they are raised about 10 inches (25cm). If you

want to raise them higher, build permanent sides.

Stones, bricks, concrete blocks, railway sleepers, logs, can all be used to make the shape. The depth is up to you and can be from 20 inches (50cm) upwards. The important thing is to provide a good root run and drainage. Even if you build on soil, drainage holes at strategic stages in the construction will help. If you build on a solid foundation, they are vital.

For the most ease in working the beds, make them about 16 inches (40cm) high and surround them with a railing you can sit on. Also make sure the beds are narrow enough so you can reach the center without walking on the bed.

Loose, coarse material such as twigs, bracken, straw, old cornstalks, etc. make a good bottom layer. A layer of good hay, fluffed so that it does not make too solid a blanket, and sprinkled with blood and bone meal or fowl pellets, or dried, shredded manure, comes next. This is lightly domed before the bed is covered with good soil mixed with compost. The more compost you can include in the mix, the better. Bought mushroom compost comes in very handy here. The bed will sink as the lower layers settle and decompose and will need topping up every now and then.

Once it is planted out, mulch well to help the soil to retain moisture. This is where a shredder is so helpful. Since the mulch is more or less on view, why not make it look as attractive as possible.

Brown twigs and small branches shredded well and mixed with green waste, make a balanced food.

CONTAINER GARDENS

If you look around it is surprising how many types of containers there are in which plants can be grown successfully. The only criterion is that drainage must be assured.

You can buy lovely ones—terra cotta, ceramic, concrete, wood, etc., but if aesthetics don't come into it you can make do with old sinks and baths, big plastic buckets and bowls (perforated) and wooden chests and cupboard drawers (perforated and standing on bricks). Ingenuity is the name of the game. I once saw a fireman's helmet in which a cucumber plant, happily bearing flowers and dangling decorously, made quite a feature hanging from the beam of a patio.

If you can make the soil provided good and rich, plants should need little more attention than an eye kept on the moisture level of the soil. One of the attractions of container gardening is that you can move containers about and alter your garden picture at will. You are also able to come to the rescue if sun, wind or rain is causing distress.

Container gardening is particularly suitable for herbs. A variety of pots of different shapes and sizes arranged near the kitchen door can look very decorative and will save a trek out into the garden when you are busy cooking. A window box allows a few herbs to be grown in an available spot too.

PLANTING OUT

The way you do it is a matter of personal choice. If you are compulsively tidy, you may have trouble with the way enthusiastic organic gardeners will have their plants jostling each other and never an inch of soil in sight.

"Nature isn't tidy" my grandfather used to say and I've quoted him on every possible occasion, not as a cop-out, but because when I first heard him say it, it was such a revolutionary thought.

Our garden at home was run with almost military precision—plants grew

Broadcasting seeds result in dense, solid stands.

Hills are small groups of seeds. Make holes as deep as the first joint on your finger.

Rows can be made with the corner of a board.

Block planting is often used in raised beds to save space

To sow small seeds, put a piece of tissue paper in a shallow furrow. Mist the tissue to keep it from blowing away. The seeds are easy to see on the tissue.

Garden Boxes

The simplest sides are made of boards. For long-lasting beds, use 3 in. (8cm) thick timber held in place with stakes. If the bed is 1 ft. (30cm) high, a cap makes a comfortable seat.

Toenail sleepers together; or drill holes through them and bolt them together. To stake logs in place, drive a pipe into holes in the log, then turn the log over and drive it into the ground.

in straight rows, the soil between them was bare and brown. There was segregation—a place for everything and everything in its place. Everything that flew or crawled was killed on sight. For me gardening was a chore and a bore, there was no fun in it. But Grandfather's garden was different and the difference enchanted me. It took years to understand exactly what the difference was and where the enchantment lay.

In the East people say as a blessing, "Go with God." My grandfather didn't know he was saying it, but his blessing was "Go with Nature."

As an experiment, try planting closer together than the seed packet or garden manual advises and then weigh up the advantages and disadvantages.

The foliage of plants growing close together shades the ground from hot sun, and pre-vents any moisture from evaporating. Warm air is trapped, protecting plants against the sudden change of temperature that comes when the sun sets. If your soil is rich in organic matter, as it surely will be once you are convinced about the good it does, there will be enough food for all.

The main disadvantage is that crowding plants together may deprive them of airflow and the resultant humidity may lead to mildew and other fungal disease. At any sign of this, spray with chamomile tea and do some judicious thinning out. The odds are though that it won't be necessary.

Good sense will dictate that some plants need room to spread—cucumbers, marrow, squash, choko, etc. so you obviously would not jostle them.

If you do like well-spaced plants of any size, make sure that the soil between them is covered with a layer of mulch.

A good study of the art of companion planting will help with planting out. You will learn which plants can live together and how far apart, which plants offer shade in which others can grow comfortably, the protection one type of plant can offer another or the threat it can offer and how far away it should be kept.

A conventional gardener seems to like the look of brown, bare, ruffled soil between the plants; a well-shredded mix of "brown" and "green" waste, neatly spread, doesn't look bad at all.

"Although all gardeners water, watering is probably the least understood of the gardener's arts. Improper watering accounts for more plant failures than any other cause."

~Author Unknown

. . . .

Watering

Knowing when and how to water is one of the arts of gardening and actually doing it correctly is one of its sternest disciplines.

Give a plant too much water and it will stifle to death because air cannot circulate in soggy soil. Give it too little and it will either collapse completely or run to seed in a panic "bolt" to try to ensure the survival of the species. An irregular supply is almost as bad because plants hate the stop-and-start syndrome.

In the early stages seeds and seedlings need a constant supply of water to get growth started, but once it is underway and roots have been put out, it has to be monitored much more carefully if the root system is to become strong and vigorous.

If the topsoil is always kept moist, the plant roots will turn upwards to the easy feed instead of pushing downward into the soil and giving the plant firm anchorage. Plant roots near the surface of the soil cannot hold the plant steady and are in danger of sun-scorch and casual damage.

Even shallow-rooted plants go down into the soil for about 12-24 inches (30-60cm) so you can allow the top inch (a few centimeters) of the soil to dry as long as it is damp enough underneath. You can easily find out how things are by poking a finder deep into the soil. Plants with taproots which can penetrate deep into the soil appreciate a good soak every now and then rather than a little and often. The trick is to water to the natural root-depth of each plant and so avoid conditions that lead to stress.

If the soil contains plenty of humus, it will hold water well and a layer of mulch around the plants will prevent evaporation, and, most important of all, stop the top layer of soil from drying out and becoming like a pie-crust which will prevent both air and water from reaching the hungry roots. As the mulch rots down, it should be gently and loosely topped up.

When you water, particularly on bare soil, do it gently—a long, slow sprinkle like a shower of rain and, preferably, before the sun has risen very far or after it has gone down in the cool of the evening. This will avoid the sudden fluctuations in the soil temperature which plants find stressful.

For some people, the peaceful evening "soak" is a pleasant time spent enjoying the fresh air and the peace of the garden after a rushed day, but it shouldn't become a regular habit; plants are like people and won't bother to try and fend for themselves if somebody else will do it for them and, like people, if they are to become strong, they have to learn to be self-reliant.

To encourage a plant to put out its own strong root system is the biggest kindness you can offer, so water generously, but only when the soil feels dry below the surface.

Hand watering with hose or watering can is time-consuming and can be tiring. Trickle irrigation solves those problems. A long perforated hose (the hole diameter can vary according to choice) attached to a tap and controlled by a timing device makes watering really easy. You can, if you think you have a memory you can trust, do without the timer, but is it worth taking the risk?

The hose can be laid out of sight under the mulch for the whole of a growing season but is easy to move should you wish to reposition it.

Water Use by Plants

Water is the life-sustaining liquid needed for the movement of materials through the plant and for the chemical processes that make the plant's food. Plants use water as a medium to transport minerals from the soil to the leaves where part of it evaporates through microscopic openings on the undersides of leaves. The evaporation of water cools the plants just as a wet towel cools by evaporation.

Water in the leaves is used in the process of photosynthesis—the reaction that changes sunlight to energy.

The plant does not transpire all of the water in its system. Some flows from the leaves, carrying sugars and other chemicals, to the flowers, fruit, growing tips and roots.

Water and Soil Type

As water is added to soil, the first 1-2 in. (5-6 cm) of soil must become very wet before the water can move to the next 1-2 in. (5-6 cm). Short waterings wet the top few inches but don't even dampen the soil below it.

Knowledge of your soil will help you water properly. Sandy soils have large pores and dry out quickly; they need to be watered more frequently. Clay soils have small pores and dry out slowly. It is easy to overwater clay soils, filling the pores and keeping the air out. If your soil isn't ideal add organic matter. Organic matter in soil acts as a sponge, holding water in sandy soils, and allowing air to penetrate clay soils. Compost is the key to all good soil.

Since the water is applied directly to the soil, you do know the plant roots are getting the benefit, but with a sprinkler, the water arcs into the air before falling on to the soil and you never quite know how much is being lost to evaporation or blown hither and yon by the wind and not reaching the plants it was intended for. There are many types of sprays and sprinklers on the market, some fixed, some movable.

When the garden is established you should be able to work out a system that fills your needs. You may have to begin with installing more taps—are there ever enough in a garden?—or repositioning others. Only you will know what will suit you best and how much you can afford to spend. If you don't mind the look of sprinklers and are not bothered about possible wastage of water, that could be the way to go. The perforated hose, which is kept out of sight and delivers water directly to the soil, is a personal preference. You can save a lot of heartache by keeping an eye on the weather signs and listening to the forecasts. A really good soaking before the onset of a dry spell can help plants to get through it without hurt.

Rain butts were once a garden feature but they are rarely seen these days, particularly not in suburban gardens. It is a pity because rainwater is so beneficial and can come to the rescue when town water is rationed. If you have room for one and are prepared to take the trouble to take the lid off when it rains and to put it back on when it stops so that mosquitoes don't use it as a breeding ground, a rain butt is worth thinking about. We have some elegant Victorian washbasins and chamber pots that we rush out whenever it rains so that we can give our big indoor plants a treat. A not-so-elegant bin catches roof run-off.

Some people save water used in laundry, bathroom and kitchen for use in the garden. If you can be sure it is free from grease, soap and detergent residue and all contact with human waste, it could be safe to use, but can you really be sure? I doubt if it is a good idea to make regular use of it but, in a panic situation, it could be of use. Then it could be a good idea to strain it through muslin or pantyhose to try and filter out any undesirable elements.

QUICK CHECK

1. Check the moisture-level of belowground soil before doing any watering by inserting a finger deep into the soil.

2. Water to the root depth of each plant.

3. Water slowly and gently.

4. Water early or late, not in the heat of the day, unless of course you can see that a plant or plants are in dreadful trouble. In that case, go to work at once and give the soil round them a good soaking. Do not let water touch the leaves.

5. Avoid overhead watering. If the weather is hot, water on the leaves will leave scorch-marks; if it is cold, water left on the leaves overnight will chill the plant and predispose it towards disease.

6. Do not water plants while they are dormant.

7. Keep water supply steady while the plant is flowering and fruiting. Too much water at this time can be as bad as too little.

8. Water under the mulch.

9. If you water the mulch, keep it from touching the plants.

Watering Techniques

Drip watering carries the water to each plant.

Quick Drip Punch holes in a tin can or hose for a simple drip system

Trench or furrow irrigation is often used in vegetable gardens. To avoid erosion of the soil, place a board under the hose when filling the trench.

An **Impulse Sprinkler** works anywhere in the garden. However, it must be high enough to ensure the water reaches over all the plants.

10. Grow plants that need constant watering near each other so that they can both benefit from your watering regime. Some people advocate growing shallow-rooted plants and deep-rooted plants close together because they take food from the soil at different levels. If you do this, and soak the soil so that water reaches the roots that go deep, be careful not to let the top layer "cake" or the shallow-rooters will suffer because their supply of air is cut-off. Lightly ruffle the surface of the soil with a hand-fork, being careful not to damage roots or stems, and keep a light covering of mulch over the soil. Keep your eye on all plants grown this way.

11. Town water supply can contain fluoride, chlorine and heaven knows how many other chemicals used to "treat" the water. I have heard that by collecting it in buckets and letting it stand in the open air for a day or two, you can minimize the effects of these pollutants. However, I have no way of checking that this is so.

Root Depths of Vegetables

SHALLOW
Cabbage. Cauliflower. Celery. Lettuce. Onion. Radish. Sweet corn.

MODERATELY DEEP
Beans. Peppers. Carrot. Cucumber. Eggplant. Pea. Squash.

DEEP
Asparagus. Globe artichoke. Pumpkin. Tomato. Watermelon.

"The honey-bee's great ambition is to be rich,
to lay up great stores, to possess the
sweet of every flower that blooms.
She is more than provident.
Enough will not satisfy, she must have all
she can get by hook or by crook."

~John Burroughs

. . . .

chapter 8

Friendly Plants and Beneficial Insects

Beneficial insects can be either predators or parasites. Predators are good bugs that eat bad bugs. Parasites are good bugs that lay their eggs on bad bugs.

You can create insect attracting habitats in and around your garden. Different insects seek different habitats, so if you set up a number of habitats, you will attract a variety of beneficial insects and when a pest comes along there will be a good chance that there will be something there to eat it.

How do you create a habitat? Plant a garden! Insects flock to flowers—not only because they are pretty, but because they also provide food in the form of pollen and nectar.

The best beneficial insect pollen and nectar providers have tiny flowers like those found on herbs. Insects tend to be tiny and so prefer small flowers because their nectar and pollen are easier to reach. They also like plants in the daisy family because the flowers are flat and give easy access to the pollen at the center.

Grow your vegetables amid flowering dill, coriander, sweet fennel, parsley, lovage and so on and see the little insects buzzing around them all the time. Or adorn your garden with a wide border of perennials and herbs. Another way to attract beneficials into your garden is to plant an "island" habitat right in the middle.

FRIENDLY FLOWERS

It's nice to see splashes of color among the green of the vegetable garden; they take away that utilitarian look given by an unbroken sameness.

There are many flowers that not only grow quite happily alongside vegetables, but also do them a power of good. The daisy family, *Compositae*, is particularly kind.

Coreopsis and cosmos, those tall elegant flowers, are rarely troubled by any pest of any disease. They grow in any type of soil, cope with any kind of weather, and whatever their secret may be, they don't seem to mind sharing it with vegetables they rub shoulders with, for plants grown near them seem to share their ability to thrive.

Santolina, lavender cotton—*S. chamaecyparissus*—is a good insect repellent in the garden and a moth repellent in the house. The shrub grows to about 24 inches (60cm) high and, if left untrimmed, becomes covered by a mass of yellow button flowers that light up the border. The silver-gray leaves are delicate and feathery.

Aster, another member of the *compositae* family, has cheerful colored flowers and, though not as hardy as some other members of the family, is an insect repellent too.

Chamomile

Anthemis nobilis, to use its botanical name, is a pleasure to grow if only for the profusion of golden flowers and elegant feathery leaves. Other plants enjoy its company. Mint becomes tastier when grown near it and ailing plants revive. Cabbages do all the better for growing near it. Onions like it—provided it keeps about 3 feet (1m) away.

Chamomile

Chamomile has been called the "plant doctor" because of its ability to encourage other plants to increase their essential oil and so taste and smell more strongly.

If you collect and dry the golden flowers, they can be used to make chamomile pick-me-up by soaking a handful in cold water for a day or two. Any young plant that looks sickly will be helped by a gentle dose of the "medicine."

Old plants can be grubbed out, chopped up and added to the compost bin to help to activate the composting process.

Larkspur and Geraniums

Larkspur and geraniums protect vines against the vine beetle.

Caterpillars have a go at geranium leaves but most other insects leave them alone, so you can grow them anywhere among the vegetables.

Lavender

Lavender gives protection against borers and mosquitoes.

Marigolds

The French and African varieties—the tagetes—are particularly useful. If you have noticed the strong whiff left on the fingers after handling them, you will have some idea why insects don't like them and why dogs, sniffing around to find somewhere to cock a leg, hastily go elsewhere.

Lavender

An edging of these vibrant little flowers around a vegetable bed will give plants protection and also look nice. If you don't like their color—and many people have a thing about orange—interplant with ageratum or any other small plants with soft blue flowers.

These marigolds give particular protection against nematodes (eelworms) in the soil and the beetle, which attacks green beans.

The beneficial effect may not be immediate. The root excretion, which the pests don't like, is produced and released slowly, but, once in the soil, it remains effective for season after season. Strawberries, eggplants, tomatoes and peppers have more hope of a healthy root system if marigolds are growing nearby.

Nasturtiums

Nasturtiums are irritatingly rampant growers, but before you succumb to the impulse to rip them out, consider the good they do.

Orange-colored nasturtiums repel aphids. If you leave them to grow under, and even to twine up apple trees, they will control the spread of the woolly aphid.

Nasturtiums grown in the greenhouse will protect more precious plants against whitefly.

Nasturtiums secrete a mustard oil, which insects find attractive and they will seek them out in preference to any cabbage, cauliflower, broccoli, brussels sprouts, kohlrabi and turnips growing nearby. It therefore makes good sense to let them wander between these crops to act, not only as groundcover to keep the soil moist, but as a decoy for insects and as a flavor-improving agent for your crops.

Marigolds

They are particularly good for giving radish a good hot taste, and for keeping away cucumber beetles.

Petunias

Grown round apple trees, petunias protect them against ants and aphids.

Salvia

Red Sage has brilliantly colored flowers that are no good at all for picking but look wonderful growing in the garden. The plants self-seed like mad and it's a good idea to accommodate them because nematodes steer clear of ground in which they
are growing.

Nematodes don't like dahlias either.

The big guns are without doubt, chamomile, marigold and nasturtium.

Sunflowers

I once saw sunflowers growing among rows of sweet corn and questioned the wisdom of it on the grounds that both were tall plants and could compete with each other for food. I was told that sweet corn is subject to attack by almost every pest you can name and that the presence of sunflowers made life easier for them. Did I not know, was the frosty question, that it was an age-old custom?

Tansy

Affectionately known as "Batchelor's Buttons," yet another member of the daisy family helps its neighbors. It is more than just a pretty face for it concentrates potassium in the soil and benefits all nearby growth. The feathery leaves and bright yellow flowers which grow at the end of the stems look good at the back of a bed of plants which need protection against cutworms, cabbage-worms and most flying insects and ants. The leaves have a strong smell and a bitter taste, but the plant is pretty. It keeps borers away from peach trees too.

Members of the chrysanthemum family are good friends too.

The Painted Daisy

C. coccineum will keep pests away from strawberries and look very pretty while doing it. Another name for it is Pyrethrum. The dust made from it is one of the insecticides that can be used safely EXCEPT that it kills bees. Fortunately bees go to bed in the evening and so you can use it without worry at dusk.

White Alyssum

White Alyssum

The tiny, sweet-smelling flowers attract tiny wasps that kill off insect pests by laying their eggs in them. The purple variety does too but to a much lesser extent. Aphids don't like it either, making it a good border for lettuce beds.

Wormwood, Feverfew

Wormwood

C. parthenium is a large aromatic plant with silver-gray leaves and small yellow flowers. It discourages fleas, flies, mosquitoes, the cabbageworm butterfly, slugs, mice, aphids. It should be kept in the vicinity of, but not close by, plants, for its root excretions are toxic and even other aromatic plants like sage and fennel can't cope with it.

It is best grown for the purpose of using the leaves to make "tea" as a pest repellent.

I never quite know what to call this plant for, as well as seeing it referred to as *C. parthenium*. *Artemesia absynthum* is another given name for wormwood, and since it is said to be one of the ingredients used in the making of vermouth and somebody told me "Wermuth" is the German for wormwood, and since wormwood is one of the ingredients of absynth—well.

HERBS AS FRIENDS

The practice of keeping herbs confined to a herb garden may suit some people, but they do so much good growing among vegetables it seems a pity to cut them off from contact with other plants. The flowers are not showy but they

Rosemary

all have a quiet charm and attract many a friendly insect to take of those predators.

Coriander

Coriander has feathery leaves and a froth of mauvish-white flowers and is an annual plant grown for its seeds. It looks quite pretty grown among vegetables where it will not only repel aphids, but also attract bees.

Hyssop

Bees love the minty flavored leaves and blue flowers of this herb, but radishes won't grow well in its vicinity. Grapevines do better with hyssop growing near them. A border of hyssop around the cabbage bed will lure the cabbage moth away.

Rue

Rue is a dainty plant with feathery leaves and golden flowers. No insects will go near it. Slugs give it a wide berth. This "herb of grace" was once used in exorcism by the Roman Catholic church. It grows easily from seed, enjoys full sun and is useful as an edging hedge, less than 3 feet (1m) high. Keep it away from sage and basil. It poisons both of them.

It is a good plant to have growing near doors and windows. Grown in a window box, it will keep flies out of the kitchen and a few plants near the barbecue area will keep them away from the food.

Rosemary

Rosemary leaves contain an aromatic, volatile oil and the cabbage moth, the carrot fly and the bean beetle don't like the smell of it at all. Rosemary can make a biggish bush but a little one, kept well trimmed, makes a pleasant edging for a vegetable bed and protects the plants growing there.

Sage

The blue-gray leaves and blue flowers make this an attractive plant, provided you don't let it straggle. It will protect carrots against the carrot fly and cabbages against the cabbage moth. Also, cabbages grown near sage are tastier and more tender than usual.

Since dried sage sprinkled round plants protects them against lice and mildew there seems no reason for the live plant not to do the same thing.

Sage grown near rosemary develops a more pungent taste.

Yarrow

Yarrow, once regarded as a weed, is now a garden favorite. It is a pleasant plant with feathery leaves and flower colors white, yellow, red and pink. There are dwarf plants and tall ones and are useful for blending among other plants where they increase the vitality of neighbors.

FRIENDLY INSECTS

Bees

Bees are great pollinators, the more of them that visit your garden throughout the year the happier and more prolific your plants will be.

Think of the flower-flavored honeys there are— clover, heather, lime-blossom, eucalyptus and so on. Other

Yarrow

honeys have the mixed flavor of all the flowers visited.

Bergamot, lemon balm, thyme, basil, sage, chives, catmint, melilot and hyssop are all herbs that attract bees.

They don't like double-flowered plants—they can't get into them easily and wormwood scares them right off, so keep that away from your herb garden.

Try to have both early and late flowering plants in the garden to keep up the interest throughout the year. Golden rod is a good late flowerer to have.

Centipedes

Centipedes, which are ginger colored and have one pair of legs to every body segment, are useful because they live on decaying garden matter, not growing plants.

Damselfly

This insect, which can be distinguished from the dragonfly by the way the wings are folded down when the body is at rest, is equipped, like the praying mantis and the assassin bug, with forelegs which are ideal for catching aphids and disposing of insect larvae. Leave it be.

Dragonflies

Dragonflies can eat their own weight in mosquitoes in no time at all—they don't sting us. They like to sun themselves on top of stakes that are taller than the surrounding plants and sit and wait. Their larvae al: eat mosquito larvae lurking in water.

Hoverflies

The insect looks like a little wasp but is silent as it hovers above plants and should not be discouraged as members of the family eat aphids and their larvae, mealybugs and grasshoppers.

Lacewings

These small green insects with four gauzy wings and golden eyes are often seen at night fluttering round an outside light. Their larvae are called "aphid-lions" because of their voracious appetite for the pests. Lacewings lay  their eggs on the topside of leaves and can easily be recognized by the thread-like stalk by which they are attached to the leaf. If you leave them be, the eggs will hatch, and the larvae, equipped with magnificent jaws, will run down the thread, immediately on the attack for their first meal. They suck the body juices of the aphids and then use the empty skins to camouflage themselves. They also eat moth eggs, caterpillars, mealybugs, scale insects and thrips.

Ladybugs

"Ladybug, ladybug fly away home
Your house is on fire and your children all gone."

I can't imagine how the nursery rhyme originated for even in early times the ladybug was a welcome visitor. Their name is a corruption of "Our Lady's bird", a name given by grateful peasants when a sudden swarm of one of the species arrived providentially and cleared up an infestation of pests that were devastating the vineyards. Ladybugs get through an incredible number

Attracting Beneficial Insects

Grow plants that give the insects food, comfort, and a place to spend the winter and they will patrol your garden.

1. Have lots of organic matter in the soil to keep your beneficial insects happy. Composted manure, for instance, not only feeds your plants but encourages predacious mites as well.

2. Try to have something blooming in your garden all the time.

3. Learn to identify your beneficial garden visitors.

4. Don't panic. If you see a pest insect, relax and give your beneficials time to work.

5. Don't use pesticides, even botanical ones. They can often kill the beneficials as well as the pests.

of aphids in a week, but also enjoy scale insects, mealybugs, leafhoppers, whiteflies, mites, the potato beetle and the bean beetle.

They penetrate among plants to places inaccessible to spray, and are the gardener's most useful insect friend. Most people can recognize them in their adult color of red, yellow or orange.

Praying Mantis

The mantis is not an attractive insect. It looks what it is—a killer. It is one of the most ferocious creatures on earth and attacks anything moving. It seizes its prey between its forelegs and tears it apart with its powerful jaws. Beetles, spiders, aphids, caterpillars, leafhoppers, bugs, your finger, if you are unwary enough to tease it, and other mantis, can fall

victim. It doesn't just kill pests, which afflict the garden, but the beneficent insects too. But, for all that, it can be useful, so it may be as well to subdue the instinct to kill it on sight. You may have seen a brown lumpy mass as big as an egg attached to a leaf or twig. These are eggs laid by the female and are waiting for the spring to hatch.

Robberfly

This ugly ferocious fly catches other insects on the wing and squirts them with its saliva to immobilize them before sucking out their body juices. It obviously must do some good for the gardener but it's up to you how you treat it.

Tachinid Flies

If you see a fly that doesn't look quite like an ordinary fly, it is probably the tachinid, which eats cutworms and caterpillars so should be spared.

A Bee Garden

Bees are great pollinators of your plants. The more that visit your garden, the more prolific your plants will be. To encourage them in your garden, plant herbs and flowers that will attract them. Here are some examples of what to plant in a bee garden.

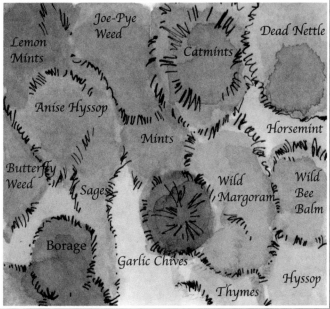

Wasps

It is better to avoid a wasp than to kill it. Yellow jacket and paper wasps eat grubs, scale insects and caterpillars. The braconid wasp injects her eggs into

aphids, and the eggs and larvae of other wasps and when they hatch out, they eat up all the fatty tissue and the host dies. There are other intricate ways in which the wasp ensures its survival as a species and they all seem to be at the expense of insects, which by and large, we can do without very happily.

Apart from exercising a useful control over pests, wasps, which are honey-feeders, help to pollinate the flower and fruit garden.

Lizards can also be helpful in deterring harmful pests.

"He had been eight years upon a
project for extracting sunbeams out of
cucumbers, which were to be put into
vials hermetically sealed,
and let out to warm the air in raw,
inclement summers."

~Jonathan Swift

chapter 9

Companion Planting

It is now widely recognized that plants, like human beings, can have their likes and dislikes and are at their best or worst according to the company they keep. The reasons why strawberries and members of the brassica family don't like each other may be obscure, but once you have seen how wretched they are together, you know there must be some cause for it.

Experts tell us it's a matter of allelopathy. This means "growth inhibition as the consequence of the influence of one organism on another." The cause of this inhibition has a lot to do with the exhalation, scents and root excretions plants make—size can also come into it—the big and strong don't leave enough food, light or air for their small neighbors. There

Tomatoes and Basil grow well together.

How Does Companion Planting Work?

Companions help each other to grow.

Companions use garden space efficiently.

Companions prevent pest problems.

Companions attract beneficial insects.

are a number of mechanisms that create beneficial plant associations.

1. Legumes, such as peas and beans, take nitrogen from the air and fix it for their own use and for the benefit of neighboring plants.

2. Some plants exude chemicals from roots, leaves or flowers that repel insects and protect neighboring plants. African marigolds are a good example—they release a chemical called thiopene, a nematode repellent—making a good garden companion for a number of plants.

3. Tall-growing and sun-loving plants can share space with lower-growing, shade-tolerant plants. This increases the crop yields from a small space.

4. Tall plants may also protect more vulnerable plants by providing wind breaks.

5. Another type of plant interaction is the beneficial habitat. The benefit comes from plants providing a desirable environment that encourages beneficial insects and other anthropods—especially those that help keep pests in check.

But whatever the reasons the results of companion planting have been obvious enough for gardeners down the years to take note of them and to come to know who the good companions and who the bad companions are.

SOME HERB COMPANIONS

Anise

A licorice flavored herb that attracts predatory wasps to prey on aphids. It deters pests from brassicas by camouflaging their odor. All plants growing near it will flourish with increased vigor.

Basil

Basil planted with tomatoes improves their growth and flavor and is helpful in repelling thrips and flies. Don't plant it near rue.

Bee Balm

Will improve the growth and flavor of tomatoes as well as attracting beneficial insects to the garden.

Borage

A good companion for tomatoes, squash and strawberries. Keeps bees and wasps away and gives nearby plants increased resistance to pests and disease.

Lettuce grows well with carrots, tomatoes, onions, radishes.

Chamomile

The German variety, an annual, improves the flavor of cabbages, cucumbers and onions. The plant also accumulates calcium, potassium and sulfur, which it later returns to the soil. Other herbs growing nearby get an increase in oil production.

Chervil

Improves the growth and flavor of radishes and keeps aphids off lettuce. Plant near dill and coriander.

Chives

If you want to improve the flavor and growth of your carrots plant chives nearby. It will also help prevent scab when planted among apple trees. A spray of chive tea will help prevent downy mildew on cucumbers.

Coriander

A good companion for dill, chervil, anise, cabbages and carrots. Repels aphids, spider mites and potato beetle.

Dill

A best friend to lettuce, it will also improve growth and health of cabbages. But do not plant it near carrots.

Dill does well with cucumbers and onions but because it attracts the tomato worm, keep it away from your tomatoes.

Fennel

Keep fennel away from peas, beans, radishes, and strawberries.

Foxgloves

Grow near tomatoes, potatoes and apples.

Dill and Carrots do not enjoy each other's company.

Garlic

Planted near roses garlic will repel aphids. It accumulates sulfur, a natural occurring fungicide, which will help in the garden. A good companion to apple and peach trees, it also deters codling moths, snails and carrot fly.

Garlic is not a good companion to peas, beans, radishes or strawberries.

Geraniums

Repels the Japanese beetle, which attacks grapevines.

Horseradish

To benefit your fruit trees and potatoes, plant horseradish as their companion.

Horehound

Stimulates growth and aids the fruiting of tomatoes.

Hyssop

A good companion for cabbages and grapes. Do not plant near radishes. Bees love it and some beekeepers rub the hive with it to encourage the bees to stay home. Radishes do not like it.

Quick Check

If you see your vegetables under attack from insects, deal with them and make a quick planting of protective plants around them to stop further attacks. If planting is impractical, place pots of suitable deterrents around the plants.

Ants—African Marigolds
Aphids—Chives, Nasturtiums
Cabbage Butterfly—Strong smelling herbs, sage, etc.
Carrot Fly—Chives, Sage
Leaf Borers—Tansy
Nematodes—Marigolds
Weevils—Garlic
Whitefly—Marigolds, Nasturtiums

Lavendar

Repels fleas and moths and the flowers attract many beneficial insects.

Lovage

Improves the flavor and health of most plants.

Marigolds

Plant freely throughout the garden. Choose the scented variety to ensure they work well.

French and African Marigolds have roots that exude a substance which spreads through the soil killing nematodes. For the best success, you need to make dense plantings.

Of all the marigolds, the Mexican variety is the most powerful of the insect repelling marigolds.

Marigolds are especially beneficial when planted with lettuce, potatoes, tomatoes, roses and beans.

Margoram/Oregano

A companion plant that will improve the flavor of both vegetables, especially cabbages and herbs.

Mint

Deters white cabbage moths, aphids and ants. It improves the health of tomatoes and cabbages when grown nearby. It also attracts hoverflies and predatory wasps. Parsley does not like it.

Nasturtiums

Protect your tomatoes, radishes, cabbages, cucumbers by planting a barrier of nasturtiums around them. It deters woolly aphids, whiteflies and cucumber beetles. It will also attract aphids and trap them. It is said that planting nasturtiums every year in the root zone of fruit trees allows the trees to take up the pungent odor of the plants. This repels bugs without affecting the taste of the fruit.

A good companion plant for cauliflowers, broccoli, kohlrabi, turnips, zucchini and apples.

Parsley

Plant among your tomatoes, chives and asparagus. It will increase the fragrance of roses when planted around the base of the bush.

Peppers, Hot

Chili pepper roots exude chemicals that prevent root rot.

Rosemary

A good companion for cabbages, beans, carrots and sage. Deters cabbage moths, carrot flies and beetles.

Parsley, onions and garlic make roses smell sweeter.

Rue

Deters beetles in roses and raspberries. It is said that it should not be planted near cabbages, basil or sage.

Sage

Used as a companion plant for broccoli, cauliflower, rosemary, cabbage and carrots, it will deter moths and beetles. Do not plant near cucumbers or rue.

Sunflowers

Planting sunflowers with sweet corn is said to increase the crop. They are also beneficial to squash and cucumbers.

Southerwood

Plant near cabbages and here and there in the garden. But keep away from potatoes.

Summer Savory

Plant with beans and onions to improve their growth and flavor.

Tansy

Plant with fruit trees—especially peaches—roses, grapes, cabbages and raspberries, but keep in mind it is not the most attractive plant and tends to be invasive.

Thyme

A good cabbage family companion.

Wallflowers grow well with apple trees.

Companion Planting Table

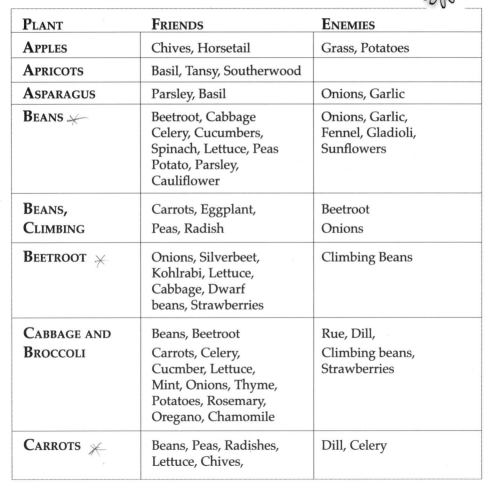

PLANT	FRIENDS	ENEMIES
APPLES	Chives, Horsetail	Grass, Potatoes
APRICOTS	Basil, Tansy, Southerwood	
ASPARAGUS	Parsley, Basil	Onions, Garlic
BEANS	Beetroot, Cabbage Celery, Cucumbers, Spinach, Lettuce, Peas Potato, Parsley, Cauliflower	Onions, Garlic, Fennel, Gladioli, Sunflowers
BEANS, CLIMBING	Carrots, Eggplant, Peas, Radish	Beetroot Onions
BEETROOT	Onions, Silverbeet, Kohlrabi, Lettuce, Cabbage, Dwarf beans, Strawberries	Climbing Beans
CABBAGE AND BROCCOLI	Beans, Beetroot Carrots, Celery, Cucmber, Lettuce, Mint, Onions, Thyme, Potatoes, Rosemary, Oregano, Chamomile	Rue, Dill, Climbing beans, Strawberries
CARROTS	Beans, Peas, Radishes, Lettuce, Chives,	Dill, Celery

PLANT	FRIENDS	ENEMIES
	Sage, Onions, Leeks, Potatoes, Tomatoes	
CAULIFLOWER	Celery, Beans	Strawberries
CELERY	Beans, Cabbage, Spinach, Dill Leeks, Tomatoes, Onion, Sage	Carrots
CITRUS	Guava	
CUCUMBERS	Beans, Peas, Radishes, Lettuce, Chives, Sage, Onions, Leeks, Potatoes, Tomatoes	Dill, Celery
EGGPLANT	Beans, Spinach	
KOHLRABI	Beetroot, Onions	Beans, Tomatoes
GRAPEVINE	Beans, Basil, Geraniums, Mulberries, Hyssop, Peas, Carrots	
LEEKS	Carrots, Celery	Beans, Peas
LETTUCE	Beetroot, Cabbages, Carrots, Marigolds, Onions, Radish, Strawberries	

PLANT	FRIENDS	ENEMIES
MELONS	Sweet corn, Radish	
ONIONS	Carrots, Beetroot, Bell pepper, Broccoli, Silverbeet, Lettuce, Strawberries, Tomatoes	Beans, Peas, Asparagus, Gladioli
PARSLEY ✳	Asparagus, Tomatoes, Sweet corn	
PARSNIPS	Peas, Potatoes, Bell peppers, Beans, Garlic, Radish	Carrots, Celery, Cabbage
PEACHES	Tansy, Garlic	
PEAS ✄	Radish, Carrots Cucmbers, Celery, Turnips, Potatoes, Peas	Onion family, Beans, Gladioli
PEPPER, BELL	Tomatoes, Onions, Carrots	
POTATOES	Cabbage, Eggplant, Watermelon, Sweet corn, Broad beans,	Pumpkin, Squash, Cucmbers, Tomatoes, Raspberries,
PUMPKIN	Sweet corn, Eggplant, Radish, Cabbage, Peas, Beans	Potatoes

Plant	Friends	Enemies
Radish	Peas, Beans, Carrots, Lettuce, Cucumbers	Hyssop
Squash	Sweet corn, Nasturtiums,	Potatoes
Spinach	Celery, Eggplant, Strawberries	
Sweet corn	Broad beans, Melons, Potatoes, Tomatoes, Squash, Cucumber	Cabbage
Swiss Chard	Onions, Beetroot, Lavender	
Tomatoes	Asparagus, Celery, Onions, Carrots, Cucumbers, Parsley, Mint, Nasturtiums	Sweet corn, Potatoes, Rosemary
Watermelon	Potatoes	

Sunflowers and Corn

"A congregation of ladybugs on a plant,
Don't invoke the old nursery saying and
ask them to fly away home... your plants
are with aphids...alive...which the ladybugs
are feeding on—and you can bless yourself
that they have come to your rescue."

~Eleanor Perenyi

. . . .

chapter 10

Pests

The pests which inhabit a garden and live off the plants growing there are legion and it's difficult to know where to start when attempting to catalog them. Some you can see at work during the daytime; others you don't see because they only come out at night or work underground; some attack leaves and stems, others roots. Some chew some suck, others bore holes.

CHEWERS AND BORERS

Caterpillars

We are all familiar with the sight of caterpillars chewing away at leaves, scalloping the edges, making holes, even reducing a healthy leaf to a skeleton. What we don't see is the moth stealthily laying the eggs that will turn into caterpillars, on the underside of the leaves.

Fightback

Caterpillars come in different colors, shapes and sizes; some you may feel able to pluck off and squash by hand—others will require to be blasted off with water and dispatched without being touched.

If you think caterpillars are around, take a first line of defense by sprinkling the dew-wet leaves with pepper. A stronger measure is to spray with derris or pyrethrum, remembering that derris is harmful to goldfish and pyrethrum to bees, so time activity accordingly. Sunlight affects the action of these two deterrents and the effect usually only lasts for about 2 days, so re-spraying could be called for.

Other good sprays to use are made from garlic, onion, wormwood or quassia.

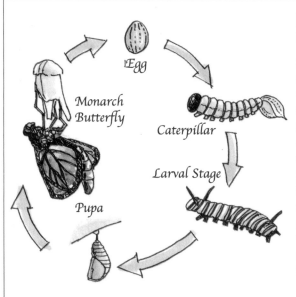

Know Your Caterpillar

One caterpillar every gardener should be able to recognize is the caterpillar of the white cabbage butterfly which is smooth and bright green. Don't spare it or it will destroy all the members of cabbage family in your garden.

Caterpillars are the larvae of moths or butterflies. To save yourself a lot of work, break the life cycle of these pests early. Attacking the larvae stage will give you peace later.

The big gun, of course, is DIPEL, the specific caterpillar poison that is harmless to every other living thing.

The bought preparation of Bacillus thuringiensis is not particularly cheap and I've been told that, since it is a living organism, you can increase your stock by mixing some of the powder with milk and leaving it overnight, and then using some of that mixed with some more milk, etc.—just like making yogurt, but I've never been in enough trouble to want to bother.

DIPEL is best used under cool, moist conditions—scorching sun would take the life out of it.

Spray it on both upper and under sides of the leaves. Caterpillars that eat leaves that have been sprayed with it will be dead by the next day.

Caterpillars are the larvae of moths or butterflies, maggots the larvae of flies and grubs the larvae of beetles.

Ants

Ants pose a bit of a problem; they feed on the larvae of insects we'd rather be without such as fruit fly and caterpillars and then blot their copy book by being over-friendly with others. They love aphids because of the honey-dew, the sweet secretion they produce, and protect them and carry them from plant to plant and thereby spread virus diseases through the garden. On the whole I think we do better without them, particularly as some are leaf-cutters.

Fightback

You can keep them at bay through their sense of smell; they hate the sharp whiff of tansy, pennyroyal and southernwood, either fresh or dried. If they persist, kill them off with a meal of marmalade laced with derris dust or spray their nest with pyrethrum or garlic and white pepper.

Birds, toads and lizards all like ants, so encourage them to visit the ant-heaps.

Beetles

Beetle

There are asparagus beetles, potato beetles, cucumber and tomato beetles, pumpkin and bean beetles, Japanese and May beetles, bark, blister and black flea beetles, and probably as many other varieties too—and all are great chewers.

Fightback

The cucumber beetle can carry bacterial wilt too, which is an added reason for getting to work with derris, pyrethrum or an extra-strong garlic spray. Try to make as much direct contact with the pests as possible.

If you come across a praying mantis, do introduce him to the bean patch—mantis love to eat bean beetles.

Cutworms

These are the caterpillars of a moth that lays her eggs by night. They spend the day under the surface of the soil or come out at night. If your young cauliflower, cabbage, beans and sweet corn collapse it probably means you've got cutworm and they've eaten through the stem below the soil.

Cutworms

Fightback

Sawdust mixed with black treacle or molasses and wetted into a "spread" will lure the cutworm out to a sticky death.

You can make a little cardboard collar for each plant. Fit round the stem and push it down into the ground so the worms can't get near. Spray soil with DIPEL before planting out.

Tansy is a pretty plant and is pretty pungent too; grown near any threatened plant it could keep the cutworm at bay. Failing that, squash a few shoots or leaves of the plant and smear the juice on the stems of the young plants you wish to protect.

Inter-planting with onions is an old-time ruse for defeating cutworms. You could try just scattering cut-up spring onion tops or onion skins around the plants.

Making Sticky Traps

The sticky trap is an effective device for monitoring pests. Many insects are attracted to yellow.

Pests drawn to the traps are unable to escape the sticky surface. Small traps resembling tongue depressors stuck in the ground or hung from plants can be used to monitor whiteflies, aphids and other pests. Larger traps, at least 30 cm by 45 cm, can be used to help control them.

For prevention, space the traps about every 12 ft. (4.5m) early in the season. Once the pest is on the plants, space your traps every 4.5 ft. (1.5m). Set the traps in the direction of the sun and at the same height as the plants you are protecting. To make your own trap, paint plywood rectangles with bright yellow enamel paint and coat the surface with 1 part petroleum jelly and 1 part liquid dishwashing detergent. It is important that the grease is clear so the insects can see the yellow color. When the trap is full of insects, clean it with vegetable oil.

If you see a brown or striped caterpillar around during the day, do deal with it so that it cannot go about its horrid work at night. Toads like to eat cutworms.

Earwigs

Earwigs

Fightback

Place rolled up newspapers or corrugated cardboard beside plants being attacked and check each day for earwigs that crawl in to rest.

Grasshoppers

You just have to pray you don't get over-run by them for, if you do, there is nothing to be done. Handpick any you see about and put down buckets of water under porch and garden lights. If you hear they are in the neighborhood and you have weed-ridden ground nearby, clean it up as fast and as thoroughly as you can. If you can, torch it in safety if the local law doesn't prohibit it.

Grasshopper

LEAF MINERS

The larvae of the little fly burrow under the surface of leaves where they are out of reach of sprays and chew away leaving white tracings, which look like scribble.

Fightback

Pick off and burn every affected leaf and spray the rest of the plant with pyrethrum. Continue picking off and spraying until you have established control.

Scale

White wax scale can be brushed off with soapy water. For complete treatment, use white oil, as directed on the container, during summer. At the later stages use 2 tablespoons of washing soda per 1½ gallons (5L) of spray mix. It is at this period that the minute young brood of scale is mobile and unprotected on the foliage.

Pill Bugs

If your young seedlings disappear overnight, suspect slaters. They are flat, gray, have a lot of legs and hide during the day. Keep mulch away from young plants as they could be holing up there. They like beer, so encourage them to drown in little caps of it. Soak some

Leaf Miner

chilies in water and spray the ground around your plants to put them off.

You could also try hollowing out potatoes and placing them near infestations of slaters as well as wireworms. They will move into the potato traps. Empty them every day into a container with a little water and kerosene.

Pill Bugs

Slugs and Snails

Domestic pets have been killed when they ate bought snail-bait and although there is now a "safe" one on the market, dealing with these pests is simple enough without having to spend money to get rid of them.

Slugs

Slugs like even ground over which to travel and have difficulty negotiating crumbly compost or a covering of bark. They betray their presence by their slimy trails that they leave behind on their night prowls. They don't like freshly-limed ground wood-ash or the bitterness left behind on the soil by watering with wormwood tea. When confronted by a slug, you can kill it by sprinkling salt over it. A kinder death can be offered by putting down saucers of beer for them to enjoy before drowning in an alcoholic daze.

Surprisingly, there is a "good" slug—the pestacella. It is pale yellow and has a small flat shell at its tail end. It feeds on other slugs and ground insects.

Snails

A morning tour of the garden after a wet night can make the handpicking of snails a satisfactory but lengthy job. Cabbage leaves left on the ground at night will offer them cover from which they can be collected and destroyed. Birds encouraged to the garden, will help to keep the population down but not low enough. Hand-to-hand combat is the most effective way of getting rid of them, and citrus skins, left inverted among the plants, will collect the pests in satisfying numbers for slaughter.

They like beer too. If you leave an empty bottle on its side in the garden overnight, by morning you will find that quite a number have slithered in and are at your mercy.

Traps

1. Broad leaves or pieces of cardboard daubed with molasses or black treacle and put down at night attracts pests which can be disposed of in the morning.

2. Leave pieces of raw potato and carrot where you want to trap wire worms.

3. Leave a bucket of water under an outside light.

4. Orange or grapefruit cups left upside down, lettuce and spinach leaves, will all attract night-feeders who will be found there sleeping the next day.

5. Shallow little containers of sugar-water, honey, beer, dried yeast, etc. will trap many pests while you sleep.

Borers

Borers are the larvae of moths or beetles. The eggs are laid at night and when the grubs hatch, they tunnel their way into the stem or root of a plant or tree branch, eating as they go. They go unnoticed until a plant starts to wilt or has stunted growth or there are signs of chewed-up bark with holes visible in branch or trunk.

Peach trees are particularly susceptible. It is said that garlic or lavender or both, planted nearby, will give some form of protection.

Corn, cucumber, melons, pumpkin and squash all suffer from borers and once they are inside the stems, the pests are safe. If you spray the soil with DIPEL before you sow or plant out vulnerable species, you are giving some protection against attack.

Borers

If a tree shows signs of the presence of borers, clean up any sawdust or detritus around it and spray each hole with a derris or pyrethrum "tea" and then plug the hole with putty. Some people try to poke the pests out, but that's tricky and takes time.

SAP SUCKERS

Aphids

Aphids go for weak and unhealthy plants, so a lot of it is up to you. If you keep up a good feeding of mulch, you should have little trouble.

When you see them, blast them away with cold water. If that doesn't work well enough, use a soapy water spray and rinse the plants with clear water afterwards. And if they just won't take the hint, try to settle the matter with garlic, nettle or wormwood spray before bringing out the big guns of pyrethrum or nicotine.

Aphids do not like the color orange, so if you have plants you wish to protect, try surrounding them with orange-colored nasturtiums that produce a mustard-oil secretion they don't like either.

Aphid

Leaf Hoppers (Jassids)

I've never felt the same about leafhoppers since someone described them as "Typhoid Marys." I knew they were a pest that hid on the underside of leaves and sucked their sap and could adversely affect many plants—beans, carrots, choko, cucumber, lettuce, melons and potatoes, for a start, but did not realize the extent to which they are disease carriers. These small, green jumping insects should be given no quarter.

Leaf Hopper

Fightback

Spray the underside of leaves with soapy water, then rinse off with clear water.

Use garlic, nettle or wormwood spray or, the final deterrents, pyrethrum or nicotine.

Mealy Bugs

Mealy bugs suck the life out of plants, but fortunately are one of the favorite foods of ladybugs.

Fightback

A spray with soapy water and a scrape-off with a knife are recommended by many experts but a brush soaked in methylated spirits applied directly to the pests, though a tedious exercise, is not only satisfying, but also highly effective.

Red Spider Mites

These are so tiny that even an infestation is hard to spot with the naked eye. They love dry and sultry conditions. They work on the underside of leaves, sucking the sap, and their presence is betrayed by a mottling, stippling and silvering of the leaf.

Mealy Bug

Fightback

Soap and water spray, with particular attention paid to the underside of all the leaves, will help. Better still, keep the red spider at bay by misting your plants in dry weather or dusting the dry leaves with sulfur powder. Plants at risk are beans, tomatoes, vines and apple, peach and pear trees.

Thrips

Red Spider Mite

You can just about see thrips—they can be white, yellow, brown or black. They make a terrible mess of the leaves of bushes and flowers, streaking them with white and since the eggs are laid inside plant tissue, they can eat out buds with impunity. Roses and carnations suffer from thrips. They also attack beans, beets, brassica, carrots, celery, cucumber, melons, onions, peas, squash, tomatoes and turnips—so if you have thrips in the garden, you have problems.

Thrip

Fightback

Thrips like weeds, so clear all weedy ground nearby as initial preventative. If you see anything you think looks like thrips, hose the plants with strong jets of water. If you know you have thrips, spray plants with a pyrethrum, derris, onion or soap spray. Ring the changes.

White Flies

We are all surely familiar with the cloud of tiny flies that rise unexpectedly when we disturb the leaves of bean, tomato and vines. They have been busy sucking the sap from the underside and are a most unwelcome sight.

They could be sign that your soil is deficient in phosphorus, so add plenty of organic matter.

Fightback

Rinse affected plants with a cold water spray. Follow that up with a soapy water one and rinse it off with clear water. Don't use detergent.

Whtie fly

If infestation persists use a garlic, nettle or wormwood spray and if even these fail, try pyrethrum or nicotine.

Scale

Scale comes in all colors, white, red, green, brown, black and the most common of these is white. The insects are covered with a colored wax that protects them from disturbance while they suck the sap and life out of plants. Birds like to eat scales, so do wasps, ladybugs and lacewings, so if you see any around, leave them be.

Scale causes new growth to wilt and leaves to drop.

Fightback

Pick off and destroy any scale you see. Better still, spray trees prone to attack with white oil—but only in the cool months of the year. With a bit of luck you will destroy the insects before they have had time to make their waxy protection. Destroy ants on sight.

Quassia, garlic, pyrethrum and nicotine sprays can all be tried. But since we don't want to destroy the insects that will destroy the scale for us, go carefully.

Paint the stems with a thick solution of clay and water.

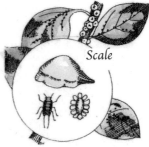

Scale

Bugs

Citrus bugs (Stink bugs), Harlequin and Shield bugs are nasty looking big things with even nastier habits. The Citrus bug eats through the fruit stem and squirts vile smelling, stinging juice—which could blind—into the face of anyone unwary enough to attempt to get rid of it without protecting the face.

A friend of mine goes into the orchard armed with a large pair of scissors. She stands well back, and reaches the leaf on which a bug is resting and cuts bug and leaf in two. A bug on a leaf stem she lifts away with the scissors and drops on to the soil and stamps on it. They are quite hard to kill and their smell makes it a very unpleasant job.

It is best to deal with them while they are in the nymph stage and small and green. They turn orange as they grow and finally black.

Harlequin, Crusader and Shield bugs are smaller. They attack citrus, grape and passion-fruit vines, vegetables, flowers and are hard to get rid of.

A bug

Fightback

If you don't feel up to a face-to-face one-to-one encounter, try spraying every day with quassia, garlic, or wormwood spray, ringing the changes. When disturbed the bugs will sometimes fly away. Clean up all debris. Tuck aluminum foil around threatened plants.

Rutherglen Bugs

Are smaller again and grayish-brown, mealy bugs are whitish. They will suck the life out of a plant if left to it. Fortunately ladybugs eat them.

Fightback

Spray with soapy water and scrape the pests off with the blunt edge of a knife. A brush dipped in methylated spirits and applied to the pests direct is a tedious exercise—often, but not always, very effective.

UNDERGROUND PESTS

Eeelworms (Nematodes)

Some of these tiny little worms do a good job in helping to break down organic matter, others attack the roots and stems of plants and weaken them very badly. They are most active in soil, so mulch heavily. Nematodes don't like marigolds, and a lot of other bugs don't like the showy little flower either so it's a must for making a border around vegetable beds.

I always understood that it was marigold roots which gave off a substance eelworms (nematodes) hated and that it made sense to plant the flowers near potatoes and tomatoes. I found that a tea made from the chopped plant, flowers, stem and leaves and poured over the ground near the plants seemed to work just as well. Maybe I was just lucky but it's worth a try.

Fightback

If you think nematodes have been attacking above the ground, put some sugar in a pan, cover with water and then boil up. Cooled and diluted, the solution can be used to spray plants in need of protection.

Even better, try a solution of molasses—that good old-fashioned black stuff— using one part molasses to 12 of water and soaking the ground with it. This can work particularly well for carrots.

If nematodes get a real hold, there is nothing for it but to give up and dig every single plant out of the patch of ground infected and to leave the soil, uncovered by mulch, open to the air, wind and rain for at least a couple of months, longer if possible.

Nematodes attack beetroot, tomatoes, lettuce, carrots, and cabbage.

WIREWORMS

Wireworms are thin and tough and about 1 inch (3cm) long. They eat seed before it can sprout, and damage seedlings and roots. You can pretty well expect to get wireworms if you have just turned grass sods over and planted above them, particularly if the drainage is not good.

Fightback

Break up the soil well; make sure drainage good. Plant radish as a trap crop. The seed is cheap and sprouts quickly. Wireworms love it and will gather round the growing plants. You can dispose of both radish and worms.

Nematode damage

FRUIT FLY

There are many ways of combating fruit fly and it's on the cards you'll be forced to try all of them.

It helps to study their breeding cycle and to work out when they are at their most dangerous.

Stone fruit suffer most from their attention but they also go for grapes, peppers, tomatoes and eggplant. If your main crops are plums, apricots, nectarines and peaches, be content with those and don't encourage the fly by having any winter or early spring fruit trees too. Particularly don't grow guava or loquats.

Fruit flies only live from about a month to six weeks. I doubt if you'll see them about. They fly and feed for less than 10 days, then mate and lay their eggs. The time to catch them is when they are on the wing. In some areas it is compulsory to take steps against the pest. Ask for advice from your Department of Agriculture.

The fly will breed in an open, badly-made compost heap which is not generating heat, so check, and speed up decomposition by a sprinkle of blood and bone or some urine.

To check whether the fly is about you could start as early as February by putting out baits. These will have to be checked regularly and replenished or replaced as needed. Small glass jars make good and not unsightly containers. Hang a good number of them, not only on the trees you want to protect but also on others nearby.

Fruit fly

Fightback

Baits can be made from a solution of vegemite or other yeast-food products; chopped banana or orange peel in water; black treacle or preferably molasses dissolved in water, bran, sugar and flour in water—anything sweet, treacly and yeasty. You can use them in open jars but if you use poisonous baits, it is best to cover them so that only fruit fly can get in. Very fine netting will do. Or you could half-fill a plastic bottle with the bait and punch holes in the empty half so that the flies can get in but will have trouble getting out. I have found that yeast dissolved in water with a dash of pyrethrum powder collected and killed a lot of them. Another way of luring them to their death is to exploit their weakness for sweet things. A strong solution of sugar and water laced with pyrethrum, splashed on and around any trees you think might be threatened in the near future can be of help. The splashing can be done with a very big old paintbrush and should be repeated every week until after the crop has been gathered. As a final touch you could do as the song says and tie a yellow ribbon round the splashed trees—the flies find yellow hard to resist.

As soon as there is evidence that they are about, hang out a McPhail trap. These will lure male flies to crawl in and die. They are not expensive. Action should be taken before fruit is more than half-ripe. They like ripe fruit in which to lay their eggs so try to make your trees unattractive as soon as fruit shows signs of ripening.

CATCHING FRUIT FLIES

You can make your own lure by using two empty soft drink bottles, and a mixture of a spoonful of honey and one of bran with enough water to form a liquid. Pour the mixture into one of the bottles. Screw on the lid. Cut the top off another bottle to form a funnel. Make a hole in the side of the first bottle large enough to screw in the funnel to form an entrance for the fruit flies. Check the lures frequently and when there is a build up—spray.

A mixture of creosote, kerosene and crushed mothballs makes a powerful repellent. Small baked bean cans with holes punched in the sides and hung up by string make good holders. Use plenty of them not only in fruit trees but also in the other surrounding trees.

Tansy, southernwood or basil planted near the trees might be of help in keeping the flies away but could never be considered total protection.

Unless you are very lucky indeed, some fruit will be affected. You will see very little to tell you so, but when you cut a fruit open, you will find a brown mess around the stone. If you catch it early, there may be minimum damage and the fruit, cleaned up a bit, could be used stewed. But all badly affected fruit should be burned so that the maggot is killed and cannot continue its life cycle. Fallen fruit should be gathered every day. If you put it in plastic bags and leave them in the hot sun for a week to 10 days, the maggots should be dead and you can use the fruit in the compost heap. I can't think why you couldn't boil the fruit up as if you were making jam and use that too. At the end of the fruiting season, clean up the ground around the trees and give it a light spray of pyrethrum.

Codling Moth

I always thought that codling moth only went for apples, and, to a lesser extent, pears and walnuts, but lately was told that stone fruit are not exempt, for a friend swore her plums and peaches were affected. She said she found caterpillars in them and that couldn't have been fruit fly.

The moths lay their eggs on both leaves and fruit—look out for black, shiny, flat pinheads—from the beginning of May. Their breeding season is short and there's another generation on the way in 6 to 8 weeks.

When the eggs hatch, the baby caterpillars make their way to the fruit and burrow into it, most often from the stem end and feed. You can often see the hole they make and the evidence of rot.

When they emerge from the fruit, after a month or more, they will take cover wherever they can to cocoon and continue their life cycle, so, at the end of the season, clear up debris of any sort, near or around the trees. No piles of twigs, no wooden boxes should be left to give them shelter.

Pile up mulch, not touching the tree trunks, nice and deep and attractive to insects and spiders, which are the natural predators of the moth caterpillar or grub as it is often called. But you will have to do more than that.

Fightback

In the summer, scrape all loose bark from around the bottom of the tree trunk and spray it with light oil. Spray again in the fall. This will stop eggs from hatching.

Make a stout cardboard collar—corrugated cardboard for preference—4-8 inches (10-20cm) wide (I like mine deep) and fit it round the base of the trunk. Give a thorough spraying with liquid derris.

After 5 or 6 days remove the collar and dead caterpillars and replace with a fresh one.

It is good to do this during summer and fall, but even better if you can keep it up longer.

Once inside the fruit, the grub is safe against sprays, so it makes sense to go for the moths and the eggs to keep the grub population down.

As with the fruit fly, baits will give you warning that the insects are around.

Hang up little jars containing a thickish solution of molasses and water all around the orchard.

When you find a few brownish-gray moths with a black spot near the wingtip, you will know they
have arrived.

As a first caution, spray the underside of the leaves with derris, and, if it is cool enough, you could give a light oil spray the following day.

As the fruit first forms, make regular inspections and pull off and burn any young fruit that shows signs of having been molested by the grubs. Be quite ruthless about this.

Keep up the baits right through the season.

Ask at your local garden shop about pheromene traps. They act like McPhail traps do on the fruit fly.

It is very much a case of eternal vigilance and continual war of attrition and because you've kept it up for one year don't expect too much success—the battle will be on again next season. But it will get easier as time goes on and you do have allies; spiders, wasps, ants, hoverflies and birds all have codling moths on their menu.

There will always be pests of one sort and another in the garden and no doubt each one has a part to play in nature's grand design, but a cultivated garden is not natural and we and they have to learn to make the best adjustment possible.

Our first line of defense is to keep the soil rich so that plants are well provided with food which contains nutrients in the right proportion and so can grow strong. Pests don't bother with healthy plants half as much as they do with weak, stunted or diseased ones, which seems a bit strange, you would think they would prefer the healthy ones; but apparently the weak ones give off an odor which is more appealing. So that when you see a healthy plant growing alongside a floppy, insect-infested one, the insects are not entirely to blame for the state it's in, they merely have taken advantage of an existing condition.

As always, it all comes back to the soil.

"Most of all one discovers that the soil does
not stay the same, but, like anything alive,
is always changing and telling its own story.
Soil is the substance of transformations."

~Carol Williams

. . . .

chapter 11

Diseases

Prevention is of course better than cure and if you keep up the organic content of the soil, feed it well, plant and water sensibly, you will go a long way towards keeping disease away.

Stop-start watering is asking for trouble; the sudden spurt in growth that comes after delayed watering results in weak and sappy stems and leaves likely to fall victim without delay.

Diseases fall into three categories—viral, fungal and bacterial.

VIRAL DISEASES

The virus betrays its presence by stunting or malforming a plant as it grows. Although I knew I should have destroyed it, I once had a plant that

I allowed to grow out of sheer fascination—it looked like something from outer space. Another telltale symptom is a mosaic pattern on leaves which can also turn yellow or roll up like a furled umbrella.

Fungal spots

Any plant that shows these symptoms should be pulled up and burned. Any garden tools used in dealing with it should be sterilized. Aphids and their pals, ants, help to spread virus around and so, to a lesser degree, do thrips. Get rid of these and you are well on your way to preventing trouble.

Seaweed spray will not act as a cure, but used regularly to feed the plants or to help them to cope with mildew, will also help them to build up resistance to viral attack.

Virus diseases are found on many weeds so keep them out of the garden and, if you have waste land or weedy patches nearby, give them a going over too.

FUNGAL DISEASES

We need a lot of beneficial fungi in the soil to work on waste matter but could well do without the ones that cause mildew and rust on leaves and rot roots and stems. The spores are microscopic and are carried on the wind and in water from plant to plant.

Downy mildew

Mildew

Powdery mildew thrives in humid conditions. It is recognizable by a film that spreads over the leaves, mostly the older ones. Cucumber, melon, pumpkin, peas and squash are its main victims.

Downy mildew thrives in wet weather.

It is recognizable by the little white tufts that appear on the leaves, most often on the underside of young ones.

Dust leaves with dry sulfur or use a sulfur spray.

Spray with chamomile, garlic, nettle or elder-leaf tea.

Pick off infected leaves on sight. If using scissors, disinfect them afterwards and wash your hands too; spores are easily transferable. Check whether the plants are too close together or if damp mulch is touching stems or leaves. Damp and a poor airflow around them make plants very susceptible to mildew.

When weather is humid, spray plants with horsetail (equisetum) tea as a preventative.

Spray with a very pale liquid made by dissolving permanganate of potash (Condy's crystals) in water.

Powdery mildew

Water the soil then gently pour over it a stronger colored solution of the above. It is a powerful fungicide and will also add potassium and manganese to the soil but unfortunately will kill worms.

Rust

Rust shows up as brown pustules or circular yellowish-brown spots on leaves. Geraniums and mint can suffer badly from it. Asparagus, beans, beetroot and Swiss chard are all affected too.

Pick off and burn discolored leaves. Make sure there is good airflow round the plant, the soil is not soggy and that damp mulch is not too close to it.

Spray with chamomile, elder-leaf comfrey or seaweed "tea."

Rot

Collar-rot, stem-rot, root-rot, damping-off of seedlings are all due to fungus which has been encouraged by an over-wet, airless condition. Get rid of affected plants.

Lighten a heavy soil with sand to improve drainage.

Check the pH. Acid soil should be sweetened. A scattering of wood-ash on the surface will help.

Brassica, rutabagas and turnips develop clubroot when grown where the soil is too acid and the fungus can thrive.

Blossom-end rot

Flowers, fruit and vegetables all suffer from fungal diseases. Part of the answer is to keep the soil rich, neutral, well drained, to ensure air-flow round plants is adequate, and to practice crop rotation.

If you grow the same type of crop in the same piece of ground year after year, you not only impoverish the soil by continually taking the same type of nutrient from it, but you also ensure the continued presence of pathogens that feed on the type of crop. See CROP ROTATION.

The Wilts

Fusarium and verticillium wilts are notable for the way they invade plant stems and cause collapse. Tomatoes are one of the main victims. When buying young plants try to get a resistant variety.

I don't think you can do much more than by keeping the environs clean and water off the plant leaves. If you remove an unhealthy plant, wash your hands before touching any of the others. On the whole it pays to be ruthless, cut your losses and start again in another spot in the garden where you can provide optimum conditions.

BACTERIAL DISEASES

Leaves develop spots and holes, shrivel and die; stems rot, twigs die, fruit rots and mummifies. If you've ever seen a pea-pod, dry, pale and shriveled or smelt a rotting ground vegetable, you will know how bad bacterial disease can be.

Clubroot of crucifers

Since the bacteria is a survivor, strong measures have to be taken. Plants ripped out and burned, tools sterilized and, whenever possible, the soil left covered with plastic for as long as you can. If you souse the soil with a good strong garlic spray, you will speed destruction of the bacteria.

If you feel you simply must make some sort of effort to save your plants, try spraying with hyssop tea, using stems, leaves and flowers.

"No sooner did I bend over and scratch
the soil with the hoe than I began to
unearth...my past. Memories
forever rooted in time were clustered in
my garden consciousness like
potatoes, waiting, crying to be dug up...
I plant flowers and vegetables. I harvest
memories—and lift."

~Nancy H. Jordan

. . . .

chapter 12

Insecticides and Sprays

There are four commercial insecticides that kill pests but do not harm animals or human beings.

COMMERCIAL SPRAYS

Derris Dust

Derris Dust is made from the roots of the plant "derris cliptica" and is sold under the trade name "Rotenone." Rotenone is a good general insecticide and can be used just dusted on plants or in a soapy water spray. Keep away from the goldfish pond though, as it is deadly to fish.

Dipel

Dipel is made from a natural bacteria—bacteria thuringiensis—and is mixed with water and used as a spray against caterpillars. As soon as you see the cabbage white butterfly, think about using Dipel.

Pyrethrum Powder

Pyrethrum powder is made from the dried flowers of pyrethrum and is a general insecticide that can be used in soapy water spray. Unfortunately it kills bees but since the effect of the spray is short-lived, you can safely use it in the evenings when the bees have retired for the night.

Quassia Chips

Quassia chips are made from the bark of a tropical tree and can be used to make a bitter-tasting tea to use as a spray against aphids and caterpillars. Luckily it does not kill ladybugs, which are natural predators of aphids.

You can buy the chips at health food stores.

Recipe for making a spray: To make a spray, boil up one tablespoonful of chips in a small pan of water then leave it to simmer very slowly for 2 hours. This will make a concentrate. Strain, cool and bottle it.

For use against caterpillars, use it diluted 1 to 4 with water. For use against aphids, dilute it 1 to 5 with water.

Ladybugs prey on aphids. If there are any around, you can still spray; it won't hurt them.

HOMEMADE INSECTICIDES

A good general recipe is to cover the selected amount of chopped material with water, bring the water to the boil and hold it there for a minute or two before removing from the heat. Leave to cool, then strain and dilute with four times the amount of water.

If you don't want to bother boiling, try covering the material with boiling water and leave it to steep for a few days, then strain and dilute until the color is really pale before using it.

GENERAL INSECT SPRAYS

Soapy Water Spray

A soapy water spray makes an excellent first-line of attack and is particularly good against aphids.

Dissolve 8 ounces (225g) plain soap (not detergent) in 2½ gallons (9L) of hot water. Stir it well to make sure all the soap has dissolved. Cool before use.

After spraying affected plants, hose them down gently with clear water. Repeat the two processes as often as necessary.

Rhubarb Spray

The leaves are poisonous to humans, so don't inhale the steam. Only make enough to use in one go. Never store it.

Chop up leaves, cover with water and boil up. Keep on a slow boil for about half an hour.

Cool, strain and add the liquid to at least an equal amount of soapy water before use.

Use your own judgment as to whether you hose it off. If there are a lot of dead insects, you will probably want to clean the plants up.

The oxalic acid in the spray soon breaks down and does no harm to any bees around.

Pyrethrum

You can use the dried flowers of feverfew (*C. parthenium*) or bought pyrethrum powder to make a general insecticide spray. Inspect the packet of powder to make sure the ingredients are natural and not synthetic and use any spray you make in the evenings after bees have gone to bed, as you won't want to hurt them.

This is one spray you must not make by boiling as the fumes could make you ill; instead, pour boiling water over the dried flowers or powder and leave to steep until cold. A little soapy water added will increase efficacy.

Don't make too much at a time and use every other day or so as its effect is short-lived, particularly when the sun is out. The spray should be pale in color.

Garlic

A garlic spray is effective against ants, spiders and caterpillars, which we don't like, but will also kill ones we do, the beneficial predators which help us out. Unless infestation is really bad, use one of the other sprays and keep the garlic one for use against cabbage and tomato worms.

Crush 4 cloves of garlic and leave them to steep in 4 cups (1L) of water for several days if you only need a small amount of spray. If you need more, soak the garlic, barely covered in vegetable oil overnight and then add, strained to 4 cups (1L) of soapy water and mix well.

Strain again and add at least 2½ gallons (10L) of water. This means you have a lot of spray. I find it tiresome to keep the soap and garlic mix bottled for dilution later and only make enough for immediate use on the garden.

Elder-Leaf Spray

Boil up a quantity of leaves in water to cover and simmer for 20 minutes. Don't inhale the steam. Cool, strain and dilute until the color is pale yellow. Use.

Oil Sprays

These should not be confused with heavy oil sprays, which are used in summer on dormant trees. The oil used is a light, mineral one.

The spray is effective against aphids, caterpillars, thrips, red spider mites, scale, whitefly and the eggs of codling moth.

Add just a little oil to some water—as much oil as one adds to a bath, you only need enough to make the spray cling to the plant and smother the pests. If infestation is bad, you can mix some pyrethrum or derris powder into it.

Never use this type of spray in hot weather—the oil could become so hot it frizzles the leaves.

 ## SPRAYS FOR APHIDS

Pyrethrum, Garlic, and Debris

All these make good sprays to use against aphids.

Nettle Tea

Nettle tea made according to the described method is good. The tea also makes a good foliar feeding spray and can be used as a liquid manure. The sludge can be tipped on the compost heap. Cut tops off nettles and leave root to grow on.

Wormwood

Wormwood makes a bitter brew that will repel flies and mosquitoes as well as aphids. Pout it over the soil if slugs are around and over the dog to help him to get rid of his fleas.

Bracken

Chopped fern left covered with water to steep for 2 or 3 days makes another effective tea.

Dilute until the liquid is pale before using it.

Lantana

It's nice to be able to find good use for that invasive pest of a bush. Make a good strong pot of tea from the leaves. Cool, strain and dilute to pale yellow in color before use.

Quassia Chips

See Quassia at the beginning of the chapter

SPRAY FOR CATERPILLARS

Dipel

The best one of all is made from Dipel (Bacillus Thuringiensis), which is a live organism and a specific for killing caterpillars. It does no harm to anything else.

Garlic Spray

Garlic Spray, made by soaking 4 or 5 crushed cloves in 4 cups (1L) of water for several days, is very effective.

An even more effective one is made by grinding together 2 cloves of garlic and 6 little hot red peppers and adding them to water made frothy by 2 tablespoonfuls of plain soap (not detergent). Use water hot enough to dissolve the soap and draw out the juices of the garlic and peppers. You'll probably have to strain the water—nothing is more annoying than trying to use a clogged spray.

Plants can be surprisingly tolerant of the temperature of the sprays you use on them, but if you use this one as soon as it is made, go carefully.

Quassia Chips

See Quassia at the beginning of the chapter

Salt

Salt is particularly good used against cabbage white caterpillars.

Mix together 4½ ounces (125g) salt and 8 ounces (225g) Soap flakes and then pour about 2½ gallons (9L) of hot water over them. Stir well until the water is as clear as you can possibly make it. Strain if you must. Spray both upper and under sides of the leaves.

SPRAYS FOR RED SPIDER MITES

Coriander Leaves

A tea made from coriander leaves, strained and left to cool before use is gentle and care must be taken to see that both sides of the leaves are thoroughly wetted. If stronger measures are needed, try derris dust.

Derris Dust

Derris Dust is not always easy to mix.

Add ½ ounce (15g) dust to 4 cups (1L) of water and stir well. Add to 4 cups (1L) soapy water and stir vigorously. Dilute with at least ½ gallon (2L) of water. Strain. Spray leaves thoroughly. This renders them poisonous to the mite.

Coriander

Salt

I've never had the nerve to try this one but the word goes that it is very effective and doesn't harm the plants. Dissolve a heaped tablespoonful of salt

in 1 gallon (4.5L) of hot water and use at once. If you do try it, it would be as well to soak the soil afterwards to disperse the salt, which could damage young and tender plants.

Onion Spray

Is very simple. Cut up onions, skin and all, and leave covered with boiling water. Use well diluted.

If you put the onions through the blender, add a garlic clove and a couple of chili peppers; cover the mush with water, strain, and dilute, you will have a spray with more oomph.

Quassia Chip Spray

See Quassia at the beginning of the chapter

Milk Spray

Use in a 50:50 solution with a little flour added to make it stick on the leaves. You can use this 3 times a week.

Anise Tea

Anise seeds are available at health food stores.

Make a good strong pot of tea with them and pour on the soil around plants on which you can see their droppings.

Nicotine Spray

This is only for use if you get really desperate and the slugs, snails, scale insects and mealybugs, etc. are getting the upper hand. Soaking about 25 cigarette butts in 1 gallon (4L) of water for 5 days will give an effective brew. I prefer doing it this way to boiling up the butts in water as the steam can hardly be healthy.
The potion must be strained before use of course. It is only effective for a day or so but it is best to leave treated plants for at least a week before picking them.

SPRAYS FOR USE AGAINST DISEASES

Bordeaux Spray

Bordeaux mixture (copper sulfate mixed with quick-lime) is a long-time favorite of the conventional gardener for the control of fungal disease. However, it kills not only the harmful fungi, but also the ones we need to have in the soil. Therefore, such care has to be taken when using it that, for an organic gardener, it is a no-no.

I tried making it at home as advised by the more knowledgeable, but lime and copper sulfate are not the most pleasant things to handle. It was tricky business and the mixture had to be used within an hour of making and then the spray kept clogging up.

I stick to simpler sprays now but for the strong-hearted, here is a recipe.

Recipe for spray

• Use a plastic watering can or bucket, not a metallic one and mix 3½ ounces (100g) copper sulfate in 1½ gallons (5-6L) of water.

• Use a similar container and mix 4½ ounces (125g) slaked lime with 1½ gallons (5L) of cold water.

• Be sure to mix both well.

Add them to each other and mix again.

This makes a lot of spray, which you may not be able to use at one go. I understand that you can use smaller amounts but knowing exactly how much of each is tricky. You are short of lime if a nail put in the mixture comes out blue.

If you really want to use the mixture, please seek more accurate information.

MILDEW

Chamomile Tea

Whenever I see mildew, chamomile tea comes to mind. Tired gardeners enjoy it too!

You can use fresh flowers, dried flowers or commercial sachets to make the tea in the ordinary way. Allow to cool and dilute until really pale in color before use.

Or you could be really lazy and leave a hand-ful of dried flowers to steep in water for a day or two.

Seaweed

This is particularly useful as it is not only effective against mildew but acts as a feed too.

Spray as a precaution whenever you think plants might be in danger i.e., they are growing very close together and the weather is humid.

You can either leave the seaweed to soak in water for a fortnight, or boil it up, well covered with water, until the liquid begins to thicken.

In both cases, dilute until it is the color of the palest sherry before using it.

Milk

Try a 50:50 milk and water spray.

Nettle Tea

Cut off the tops of any plant you find and leave the roots to grow on.

Put stems and leaves in water to cover and bring to the boil. Hold for about 10 minutes. Cool, Strain. Dilute to the color of weak tea before use.

Chive Tea

Use bought dried or fresh chives and cut finely to make an ordinary pot of tea. Let it stand until cold. Strain and use at half strength.

Horsetail (Equisetum) Tea

This is a good weed to have in the garden.

The stems are thin and wispy and the head looks like a tiny asparagus. It is not an attractive plant and will invade any dry and stony spot in the garden and refuse to leave. The roots make it hard to pull out and the spores are carried on the wind.

If you don't have any, you will probably be able to buy it, dried, at your local health store for it has good medicinal use too.

Boil up a tablespoonful of dried leaves or a handful of fresh ones in 4 cups (1L) of water and hold at the boil for 20 minutes. Let the liquid overnight or even longer. Strain before use.

The liquid will be rich in silica, vitamins and minerals so any you have left over can poured on the soil.

FRUIT ROT

Spray with chamomile tea every day and garlic and seaweed every few days.

FUNGAL DISEASE

Spray with chamomile tea at the first sign of trouble. Milk, elder and horsetail tea can be the second line of attack.

See Aphids for elder tea and Mildew for milk and horsetail sprays and Bordeaux spray.

RUST

Chamomile, elder, seaweed and comfrey tea are all recommended.

"Ripe vegetables were magic to me.
Unharvested, the garden bristled with
possibility. I would quicken at the sight of
a ripe tomato, sounding its redness from
deep amidst the undifferentiated green."

~Michael Pollan

. . . .

chapter 13

Growing Vegetables

By following the soil management practices we have outlined earlier in this book, supplemented with a variety of cultural practices, you should be growing wonderful crops.

It is important to select seed carefully. Where possible, obtain seed (or plants) from an organic grower; it should have a strong constitution and resistance built into it from the way in which it was produced. Saving your own seed will ensure that the quality of your crops is consistent.

CROP ROTATION

A second cultural practice, still surviving from the last century, is that of rotation of crops. Plans for rotation can

be many and complicated, but basically the essence of rotation is "don't plant a crop in the same place two years running." By doing this, you prevent the establishment and increase of a particular disease or pest in the soil, and you avoid the occurrence of nutrient shortage, brought on by a vegetable that needs a particular mineral.

Originally crop rotation was invented to prevent clubroot of cabbages infecting the soil. All the cabbage family are prone to infection and it was quite possible for the whole soil to become contaminated.

To make rotation simpler, vegetables can be divided into three groups: the cabbage family and leaf vegetables; the root crops; and potatoes together with peas and beans. These divisions take into account the organic matter and food needs of the plants, too, since cabbages and their relatives on soil dressed with organic matter the previous autumn, and limed in winter. Root crops should follow another crop that grew in manure-treated soil the previous season, and potatoes do best on soil containing organic matter worked in shortly before planting, as do the legumes. A further refinement for the root crops is that lime should not be used, but they do like potash, so wood ashes or rock potash should be mixed in.

The legumes put lots of nitrogen in the soil, which benefits leaf crops so it makes sense to put them in after a crop of peas or beans. Follow the leaf crops with tomatoes and other fruiting vegetables and then put in the root crops. I think it wise to follow the root crops with a fallow season, leaving the bed manured, composted and mulched, but empty; or grow a green manure crop.

You can vary your plan, for instance, early carrots or beets can fill in the spaces waiting for brassicas, and if you want main crop carrots to be sown late in early summer, lettuce or broad beans can fill the space in spring. Crops like asparagus and artichokes, being permanent, do not form part of a rotation. But whatever you do, follow the principle of ✗ planting different successive crops in the one site, even if it is a case of only moving a row or two away.

ASPARAGUS

If you are very patient, you could grow asparagus from seed, but you would have to wait until it flowered to know which plants to grow on. Females do not crop as well as the males. Most people buy one-year-old male crowns.

Asparagus needs a cool shady spot. In hot areas, trench growing should be considered.

Sprinkle the ground with lime, put down a thick layer of good mulch with some organic fertilizer mixed through it and set out the crowns about 20 inches (50cm) apart. Cover with a thin layer of compost and then cover that with an 8-inch (20cm) or more

layer of looser mulch; hay or seaweed are particularly good. Sprinkle the bed with a little more lime and some dried chicken manure and water it well. It is important to keep a deepish layer of mulch over the plants.

A little blood and bone will help them in the early stages, but after that, all they should need is water and more mulch. Keep the water supply regular.

Begin to pick when the stems are long, fat and white, but don't over-do it in the early years. Give the plants time to mature. The stems should be snapped off close to the ground.

Varieties

Mary Washington, Martha Washington, Dutch Purple

Good Companions

Tomatoes, Parsley, Basil, Bell Peppers, Nasturtiums, Lettuce

BEANS

Since beans can grow in the same spot year after year, you could erect ✗

a permanent tepee for them to grow over or train them up wire strung between two posts. Choose a spot out of the wind.

Dwarf French beans do not require support, but will appreciate being able to lean against hay stuffed around them.

Incorporate mulch laced with organic fertilizer (blood and bone, old chicken manure, Dynamic Lifter) into the soil then top it with a thinnish layer of good compost and sow the seeds in it 1 inch (2.5cm) deep and 6 inches (15cm) apart. A dozen seeds round a tepee or 10-foot (3m) row make enough for a first crop. Sow a second one nearby when the plants have about four strong little leaves. Do not soak the seeds before planting. Watch the weather and do not sow if heavy rain is on the way.

Mulch well as they grow, preferably with compost. Water sensibly and don't let the ground puddle. Start picking early to encourage the plant to produce more beans.

Broad beans are heavy feeders and strong growers, so growing them in a trench has its points. Ruffle up the soil at the base and incorporate some lime before putting down a layer of mixed mulch and fertilizer and some compost in which to sow the beans. Mulch well as they grow and water by allowing the hose to trickle into the trench. A little weak liquid manure when they start to flower will be appreciated. Frost will nip the flowers so adjust sowing time accordingly. Beans take from 2 to 3 months to mature. Never plant beans near onions, garlic or fennel. They like the company of beetroot and potatoes.

The handsome Scarlet runner bean only grows well in a cool climate.

Varieties

Dwarf Beans: Hawkesbury wonder, Royal Windsor, Pioneer, Brown Beauty

Climbing Beans: Epicure, Purple King

Runner Beans: Scarlet Runner,

Improved Tendergreen

Broad Beans: Aquadulce, Bonnie Lad, Primo

Pests and Diseases

Dwarf, Runner and Climbing Beans:

1. Aphids, Bean beetle fly

Hand pick or blast off with a water-spray.

If necessary, spray with garlic.

2. Red spider mites

Leaves become mottled, stippled and silvered

(a) Mist your plants in dry weather; the mites like parched and dusty conditions.

(b) Spray with 50/50 milk and water.

(c) Spray both sides of leaves with coriander tea.

(d) Dress the soil with wood-ash.

(e) Pour comfrey tea over the soil near the plants.

Broad Beans:

1. Aphids and Caterpillars

Handpick and destroy on sight. Aphids carry viral diseases and caterpillars chew.

Putting pepper or curry powder on the leaves will make them less attractive to caterpillars.

2. Rust

Dust leaves with sulfur powder. If persistent, see Rust in Pests and Diseases section.

3. Botrytis

The chocolate spots on the leaves look nasty but a plant is usually able to hold its own. Pick off as many leaves as seems sensible.

Good Companions

Carrots, Cucumber, Cabbage, Cauliflower, Lettuce, Peas, Parsley, Spinach, Marigolds Dwarf beans especially like Beetroot and Potatoes.

Bad Companions

Onion, Garlic, Fennel, Gladioli, Sunflowers

BEETS

Beet don't like either frost or hot weather, but provided the plants are given a little protection in the one case, and considerate watering in the other, seem able to cope reasonably well. They tolerate shade.

Put down a loose mulch of hay, stems, etc. and scatter lime through it.

Add a layer of thicker mulch topped with a thin layer of compost and sow seeds that have been soaked overnight as thinly as you can.

As seedlings grow, thin out to 2 inches (5cm) apart and mulch between them and from here on, keep the mulch and soil damp—if you stop and start, you'll get woody beetroot. During the 10 to 12 weeks of growth to maturity give occasional doses of weak liquid manure or seaweed emulsion.

They are quite good-tempered plants and you can tuck seedlings among onions, lettuce, Swiss chard and cabbage. Never let fresh manure get near them though.

Varieties

Early Wonder, Burpee's Golden, Detroit Dark Red, Ruby Queen, Little Ball

Pests and Diseases

Maybe mildew

Pick off affected leaves and sprinkle the rest with powdered sulfur.

Good Companions

Onions, Swiss chard, Lettuce, Cabbage, Dwarf Beans

BRASSICA

Cabbage, cauliflower, brussels sprouts and broccoli all like cool weather, lime in the soil and decayed, but not fresh, manure. They become sappy if given too much water and rot if crowded with damp mulch. Dry sawdust used as a mulch will deter slugs and snails.

Cabbage take from 2 to 4 months to come to maturity, broccoli and brussels 3 to 5 months and cauliflowers 6 months, so plan for growth during the coolest time of your region.

CABBAGE

Lime the soil before putting down a layer of loose mulch. Cover it with denser mulch, enriched with blood and bone, rotted manure or bought organic fertilizer and top it with compost. Then sow seeds or plant seedlings, making the spacing suitable for the size of the type chosen. If you use dry sawdust as mulch, water underneath it gently and regularly and give a dose of weak liquid manure every now and then.

Cabbage hate being near strawberries or tomatoes but don't mind beans, beets, celery, onions and potatoes. The scent of rosemary, mint, sage and chamomile will deter pests. Don't plant cabbages in the same spot in subsequent years or you could get clubroot. If you must, bury short sticks of rhubarb in the soil around the plants and hope for the best.

Varieties

Early: Green Cup Hybrid, Sugarloaf, Early Jersey Wakefield

Late: Danish Ballhead, Late Flat Dutch

Year round: Ballhead, Sugar Bowl

Pests and Diseases

1. Cabbage white butterfly

Dust plants with derris to keep insects away

2. Cutworms

Protect seedlings with a little cardboard or tin collar pushed well down into the soil around them. Spray with Dipel

3. Nematodes

If plants are weak and have knobbly roots, there are nematodes in the soil. Soak the soil round the plants with tea made from French marigold plants, roots and all. Or plant a border of marigolds around the bed.

Make the plants little tin or cardboard collars and push them deep into the soil round them.

4. Slugs and snails

Surround plants with gravel, grit, smashed eggshells, etc.

Put down traps. See Pests and Diseases.

Good Companions

Beans, Nasturtiums, Beetroot, Celery, Mint, Thyme, Sage, rosemary, Dill, Potatoes, Chamomile, Oregano

Bad Companions

Rue, Parsnip

CAULIFLOWERS

These are heavy feeders so add more dried manure, blood and bone or bought organic fertilizer than usual to your prepared bed. Dynamic Lifter did wonders for mine.

Set seedlings about 18 inches (45cm) apart. Water well and start to mulch as soon as growth is established. Keep the soil under the mulch damp but not wet.

As the heads form, close the leaves over them—this will help to keep them white. Cauliflowers grow well in trenches.

Varieties

Check with local nursery for best type for your locality.

Good Companions

Celery, beans, thyme, nasturtiums, sage

Bad Companions

Strawberries

Pests and Diseases

1. Cabbage white butterfly

Dust plants with derris to keep insects away.

2. Cutworms

Protect seedlings with a little cardboard or tin collar pushed well down into the soil around them. Spray with Dipel.

3. Nematodes

If plants are weak and have knobbly roots, there are nematodes in the soil.

Soak the soil round the plants with tea made from French marigold plants, roots and all.

Plant a border of marigolds around the bed.

Make the plants little tin or cardboard collars and push them deep into the soil round them.

4. Slugs and snails

Surround plants with gravel, grit, smashed eggshells, etc.

Put down traps. See Pests and Diseases.

BRUSSELS SPROUTS

Grow these in a shallow trench. Scratch up the soil and incor-porate some lime, then half-fill the trench with really good compost. Plant about 30 inches (70cm) apart. Add more compost as they grow and give regular gentle feeds of liquid manure. At the first sign of mildew, spray with methylated spirits. If the weather gets too warm, protect them by a loose mulch of hay.

Varieties

Top Score Hybrid, Lunet Hybrid, Jade Cross, Long Island, Prince Marvel

Pests and Diseases

1. Cabbage white butterfly

Dust plants with derris to keep insects away.

2. Cutworms

Protect seedlings with a little cardboard or tin collar pushed well down into the soil around them. Spray with Dipel.

3. Nematodes

If plants are weak and have knobbly roots, there are nematodes in the soil.

Soak the soil around the plants with tea made from French marigold plants, roots and all.

Plant a border of marigolds around the bed.

Make the plants little tin or cardboard collars and push them deep into the soil round them.

4. Slugs and snails

Surround plants with gravel, grit, smashed eggshells, etc.

Put down traps. See Pests and Diseases.

Good Companions

Sage, Hyssop, Thyme, Nasturtiums

BROCCOLI

Most people buy seedlings—a punnet gives a good supply.

Prepare the ground as for cabbage; set out the plants allowing 20 inches (50cm) of space all around each one. Water well and keep the plants growing steadily. Use a loose mulch so that air can get round the stems and water under it, giving regular doses of liquid manure. Broccoli likes food. When the central head develops, nip it out to encourage the plant to put out side-growth.

Varieties

Waltham 29, DeCicco, Calabrese, Green Duke, Liberty, Skiff, Arcadia

Pests and Diseases

1. Cabbage white butterfly

Dust plants with derris to keep insects away.

2. Cutworms

Protect seedlings with a little cardboard or tin collar pushed well down into the soil around them. Spray with Dipel.

3. Nematodes

If plants are weak and have knobbly roots there are nematodes in the soil.

Soak the soil around the plants with tea made from French marigold plants, roots and all.

Plant a border of marigolds around the bed.

Make the plants little tin or cardboard collars and push them deep into the soil round them.

4. Slugs and snails

Surround plants with gravel, grit, smashed eggshells, etc.

Put down traps. See Pests and Diseases.

Good Companions

Sage, Chamomile, Celery, Nasturtiums

PEPPERS

Bell Peppers (mild)

Chili Peppers (hot)

Peppers need four months of warm weather to bring them to fruition, so estimate planting time accordingly.

Chili peppers cope with extreme heat better than the Bell ones do. If the temperature shoots 85°F or more (30°C or more), give your bell peppers shade.

One chili bush—which is quite ornamental—will probably be enough as they are very good and constant croppers.

You can grow peppers from seed, but it's a lengthy business and most people buy seedlings. They like humus-rich soil, not only because it contains good food, but also because it drains well. Incorporate compost into the soil before planting out.

Plant about 20 inches (50cm) apart and it's a good idea to put in a short stake with each one as they don't like wind and may need help to hold up when the fruit forms.

When they are growing well, give them a dose of weak liquid manure and mulch well. A loose hay mulch gives protection against wind and allows you to water through it. It is important to water regularly, but always keep moisture away from the leaves and stems and don't let damp mulch touch them either.

If you have made the soil rich, extra feeding should not be needed except for a small dose of weak liquid manure when you can see fruit is forming. Too much nitrogen will produce lush leaves but not much fruit.

You can pick bell peppers and hang them up to ripen provided they are in a clump of soil.

Varieties

Sweet: Giant Bell, Californian Wonder, Golden Bell, Sweet Cherry

Hot: Long Red, Hungarian Yellow, Serrano

Pests and Diseases

1. Aphids

Pick off. If using a water-jet to displace them, go gently as the plants are shallow-rooted.

It is important to keep peppers free of aphids as they carry viral disease from plant to plant.

2. Cutworms

3. Fruit fly

4. Viral disease

Buy a resistant variety.

If plant becomes stunted or deformed and the leaves peculiarly patterned, rip it out and burn it.

Disinfect any equipment used. And hands: If you smoke, wash your hands before going near the garden.

If you feel the need to protect the plants in advance, spray with seaweed emulsion.

5. Mildew

6. Brown spot

If leaves and fruit start to develop brown spots, spray at once with horsetail tea.

Good Companions

Eggplant, Nasturtiums, Basil, Parsley

CARROTS

Carrots do not like too much heat. In the warmer areas, it is wise to give them partial shade. They like a rich friable soil that holds water well, but is loose enough to allow the roots an easy downward run. If you have a heavy soil, it is quicker to build a new bed on top of it than to dig it over and add sand etc, to lighten it.

Prepare the bed by putting down a loose mulch of hay, chopped corn and bamboo stalks, coarse leaves, etc. Sprinkle with some blood and bone, dried manure or bought organic fertilizer. Cover with a good layer of mulch and top with another shallower layer of compost. A few crumbled mothballs mixed in will deter the carrot fly.

Sow seed sparingly in spring and thin out plants to 30 inches (75cm) apart, disturbing the soil as little as possible. Water well and keep mulch around the growing plants so the soil cannot dry out. Old sawdust is good. As soon as the plants are growing well, make a second sowing.

Leeks and carrots sown in the same row—more carrots than leeks—will protect each other from insect attack. Sage onions and chives planted nearby also protect carrots.

Varieties

They come in different sizes and shapes. Short and fat, thinner and longer. The information is on the seed packets.

Good Companions

Dill, Onions, Leeks, Lettuce, Sage, Peas, Radishes

Bad Companions

Tomatoes, Parsnips

Pests and Diseases

1. Aphids
2. Nematodes

Don't plant carrots in this spot for the next few years.

CELERY

Celery is a marsh plant and likes an acidic soil, good food and plenty of water.

Dig a trench elbow-depth and half as wide and half-fill with compost to which you have added a little peat. Since seed takes so long to germinate, use bought seedlings and set them out 8 inches (20cm) apart at a time when you know you have 4 to 5 months of warm weather ahead. If you only have a little compost, use mulch mixed with dried pig manure and top that with compost. Mulch generously but loosely as the plants grow and keep the soil moist by trickling water into the trench. If you want really white celery, wrap the well-grown stalks in newspaper, just leaving the leaves emerging. Green celery will have more vitamins, but white is crisper.

If you plant celery and leeks in alternation, you will have happy plants—they both like pig manure.

If the compost-grown plants are slow-growers, feed with liquid manure once a week.

Pests and Diseases

Watch out for aphids, slugs and snails

Good Companions

Beans, Tomatoes, Leeks, Thyme

CHINESE CABBAGE

It is wiser to think of this as lettuce rather than as cabbage for it has the same willful tendency to bolt if things are not to its liking. It looks like a coarse lettuce too but has a more pronounced flavor.

It has to be grown quickly, without any setback and does best in the cooler areas of the country.

Where it is warmer, try sowing towards the end of summer so that the plants are maturing as the weather cools. The plants take about 10 weeks to be ready to pick, so you can stagger planting to suit your needs and area.

Sow pinches of seed 12 inches (30cm) apart and thin out the weaklings as the plants grow. Don't bother to transplant anything you take out.

Water steadily and regularly, keeping the soil moist but not soggy. Protect the plants with a loose mulch and always water under it. A feed of liquid manure (See Fertilizers) will please them.

Varieties

Wong Bok, Pe-tsai, Hong Kong Hybrid, Seppaku, Jade Pagoda

Good Companions

Lettuce, Potatoes, Onions

Pests and Diseases

Slugs and Snails

CUCUMBER

Cucumber is a vine, so it can be trained to grow against a fence or trellis. If you grow it along the ground, give it the support of some crumpled chicken wire.

They need plenty of water but good drainage, warmth for the 2 to 3 months of growth and good soil. If you don't have enough compost, add some well-rotted manure or blood and bone or bought organic fertilizer to the soil.

Half a dozen bought seedlings should be enough. Set them out 20 inches (50cm) apart in a small depression made in the soil so that water can be directed to the roots. Don't water overhead as wet leaves are prone to mildew. If you see any signs of it, spray at once with nettle or chamomile tea. The plant has male and female flowers so in the absence of bees, you will have to hand-pollinate. Add compost or mulch enriched with a little fertilizer as the plants grow and start picking the cucumbers when small to encourage the plant to produce more. Be sure to water regularly.

If you plant radish among them, the cucumber beetle will be discouraged. Potatoes, beans, celery and lettuce make good companions too.

Varieties

Marketmore 70, Green Gem, Sweet Success, Burpless Hybrid, Crystal Apple, Sweet Slice

Good Companions

Nasturtiums, Potatoes, Beans, Celery, Lettuce, Sweet Corn, Cabbages, Radishes, Sunflowers

Bad Companions

Potato, Tomatoes

Pests and Diseases

1. Aphids
2. Red spider mites
3. Nematodes
4. Mildew

EGGPLANT

Eggplants are very tender perennials that need three or four months of warm weather to help them to fruit well. Don't sow or plant out seedlings till the soil has warmed up in spring. Bought seedlings are less trouble and less wasteful as the average family will need only 7 or 8 plants.

They like a rich neutral well-drained soil and plenty of sunshine.

If necessary, ruffle up the soil and add some compost before planting to give plants a good start.

Set seedlings out 30 inches (75cm) apart with a small stake beside each of them as the fruit is heavy and they are almost certain to need support.

Keep plants well mulched, particularly when the weather is hot. Water heavily and frequently, making certain each watering drains away and be certain to keep damp mulch from touching the plants. If the sun becomes fierce, protect them. A very loose hay mulch will do.

Pick before the skin starts to wrinkle.

Varieties

Black Beauty, Supreme, Long Tom, Long Purple, Black Gnome, Moneymaker

Pests and Diseases

1. Caterpillars
Hand pick; spray with Dipel
2. Aphids
Hand pick; blast off with water
3. Red spider mites
Avoid dry and dusty conditions round plants
4. Cutworm
5. Mildew
Pick off affected leaves and spray the plant with chamomile tea

Good Companions

Beans, Bell Peppers, Lettuce

Bad Companions

Potatoes

LEEKS

✳ Leeks are reasonably frost-tolerant but plant so as to give them 4 to 5 months good weather in which to grow. They flourish best where temperatures seldom go above 75°F (25°C).

Dig a 6-inch (15cm) deep trench in a sunny spot, half-filled with compost.

Set out seedlings firmly in the soil 6 inches (15cm) apart and water well. As the plants grow, add more compost or mulch enriched with organic fertilizer. Keep the soil moist but not wet. When plants are tall and strong, mulch around them with hay or other loose mulch, leaving just the tops of the leaves above it. This will help to blanch them and protect them if necessary.

Protect them from frost with loose straw.

Varieties

Giant Musselburgh, American Flag

Pests and Diseases

1. Onion fly
Grow near carrots

LETTUCE

Lettuce prefers cool weather, can take dappled shade, but must be grown quickly and steadily. It takes around 8 weeks to reach maturity, so by making sparse, regular sowings from early spring onward, you can have a constant supply.

Add compost or well-rotted mulch to the soil, water, then sow seed as thinly as possible in very shallow drills and cover lightly. Thin when growing well—large types naturally need more space than small ones. You can use the thinnings if you are very careful.

As they grow, keep them well watered and loosely surrounded by light mulch of well-rotted leaves—some people use sawdust to deter slugs and snails.

They will bolt if subjected to too much heat and too little water.

Varieties

Ithaca, Burpee Iceburg, Cos, Webbs, Great Lakes, Imperial, Buttercrunch, Mignonette, Regency Red, Oak Leaf, Punnets of mixed-type seedlings.

Pests and Disease

1. Aphids

2. Slugs and snails

3. Cutworm

4. Viral disease

If veins of the leaves become pronounced and the leaves ridged, pull up the plant and destroy it at once. Do not grow lettuce in this spot for at least 3 years.

5. Downy mildew

6. Root-rot

Good Companions

Carrots, Onions, Strawberries, Beetroot, Cabbage, Radish, Marigolds, Borage, Chervil

MELON

Melons take up space but are quite easy to grow. They could be trained over a trellis but the weight of the fruit makes giving support on the ground a better proposition.

They need from 3 to 5 months of warm weather to come to fruition, so judge planting time according to your area and the variety chosen.

Since you will only need 2 or 3 plants, you can save the seed from a bought fruit and I have often found seeds sprouting in my mulch or compost.

Enrich the soil with compost or well-rotted mulch mixed with organic fertilizer and keep watering regular and plentiful as the plant grows, taking care not to wet the leaves as mildew could be a problem. If you are unfortunate, give a light spray with methylated spirits at once. Supporting the vine on chicken wire covered with a springy mulch will help to keep air moving around the plant, and though many people feel straw looks untidy, it can be invaluable.

There should be plenty of feed in your prepared bed, but an occasional dose of liquid manure will be helpful.

Let the fruits ripen on the vine. Watermelon will sound hollow when tapped, and it's easy to tell when rockmelons are ready as the stem weakens and becomes easily separable from the fruit.

Varieties

Rockmelon, Honey Dew, Hale's Best Watermelon , Candy Red, Hawkesbury, Sugar Baby, Sunnyboy, Yates Early

Pests and Diseases

1. Cucumber beetle
Pick off on sight, it can carry virus diseases
2. Red spider mite
3. Mildew

Good Companions

Sweet Corn, Sunflowers

Bad Companions

Potatoes

Note: When the plant has finished fruiting, pull up, chop and add to the compost heap. The leaves are good food value.

ONIONS

There are early, mid-season and late maturing types, so study seed-packet information. They take about 7 months to come to maturity.

The ground must be well prepared and the soil rich as feeding during growth will encourage leaves but not the bulbs. Slash any weeds and cover the ground with a layer of crunched-up newspaper.

Cover that with a coarse mulch of hay, chopped stalks, thin chopped twigs etc. and sprinkle with some blood and bone, dried chicken manure or bought organic fertilizer. Then add a denser mulch of old grass clippings, rotted leaves, chopped weeds, old veggie leaves, etc. and top with a good layer of compost. Sprinkle the surface with a little more food, water until nicely moist but not sloppy and then plant seeds or seedlings.

The plants should grow about 6 inches (15cm) apart. Do not mulch them.

The stems should stay slender enough to bend over easily as the bulbs ripen. Any thick-stemmed ones should be removed at once.

The bulbs should be kept just above the soil and allowed to dry off before picking. Seed for salad onions can be sown in succession throughout most of the year.

Onions grow well near carrots, beetroot, Swiss chard and lettuce, but will inhibit the growth of peas and beans.

Varieties

Yellow Globe, Early Yellow Globe, White Portugal, Sweet Spanish, Early Berletta, Hunter River White, Hunter River Brown, Gladallan Brown, Early Flat, Early Grand, Odorless, Mild Red, Cream Gold, White Imperial, Spanish, Brown Spanish

Pests and Diseases

1. Onion fly
Plant near carrots
2. Thrips
3. White rot

If onions become soft and covered with fungus, get rid of them and improve the drainage of the bed.

4. Downy mildew

Good Companions

Lemon balm, Borage, Carrots, Beetroot, Silver beet, Lettuce

Bad Companions

Peas and beans

SPRING or SALAD ONIONS

You can sow these in most places in the country more or less all the year round. Seed packets give the specific instructions needed.

Sow thickly, 1/2 inch (1cm) deep in drills, in good but not rich soil. Keep growth steady by regular watering.

You can then either keep snipping off the tops for use in salads etc. and leave the bulb growing in the soil or thin the rows by digging out whole little plants.

Varieties

White Bunching, Beltsville Bunching, Evergreen White

PEAS

Peas are cool weather plants and need lime in the soil, which must be rich and well drained. You can grow early and late crops of both climbing and dwarf types. Climbing peas need the support of a fence or trellis. Crumpled chicken wire or a heavy mulch of hay will give dwarf peas support. Good rotted mulch or compost added to the soil will give the plants a good start. They take from 2 to 4 months to mature, so judge planting time accordingly. Sow seed 1 inch (2.5cm) deep, and space out to give reasonable room for dwarf peas to spread and about 3 inches (7cm) apart if growing up a trellis. Mulch and water well as they grow. Start picking when the pods are beginning to plump up.

Do not soak seed before planting or sow if heavy rain is forecast.

Snow Peas

The snow pea is an annual, cool-climate plant—it won't germinate in heat. There are both climbing and dwarf varieties. The climbers can reach 7 feet (2m) in height—the dwarf 3 feet (1m). They both need support—wire netting does well in both cases.

Sprout the seeds before planting out from autumn to spring in temperate areas—from spring to autumn where it is colder. Give about 10 weeks of good weather for the peas to be ready to pick. They like a compost-rich soil with a scattering of wood ash to supplement the potash. Water regularly and make sure the soil does not puddle. Eat within a short time of picking to enjoy them at their best.

Varieties

Early season: Freezonian, Little Marvel, Dwarf, Earlicrop, English Wonder, Little Wonder

Mid-season: Greenfeast, Giant Stride, Sugar Snap, Telephone

Late season: Alderman, Lincoln, Wando

Climbing: Telephone

Pests and Diseases

1. Aphids
2. Red spider mite
3. Birds

Just do what you can with netting and other deterrents but be prepared to lose some.

4. Mildew
5. Rot, wilt and blight

Choose resistant strains. Pull out any affected plants and destroy.

Note: It is important to keep the environs clean and free from rubbish. Never handle the plants when they are wet.

POTATOES

When you read the list of problems you can have when growing potatoes, you could be put off. I was and decided not to waste too much time, effort or ground on them. After all, spuds are cheap enough to buy.

We still laugh when we talk about that first crop.

I've never taken less trouble with anything. I threw down some newspapers, covered them with a good layer of compost, scattered the potatoes around, some of them not even showing sprouts, covered them over with a loose mulch of hay, scattered some dried chicken pellets among it and some wood ash—because I'd read somewhere that potatoes like potash, watered well—and left them to it. All I did from then on was to fling mulch over the growing stems so that all to be seen was the top of the leaves. By poking a finger under the mulch every now and then I could tell if water was needed and found it no problem to keep the bed gently moist. Out of curiosity, we fished out some tubers when the flowers started falling. From then until the tops completely died off and the whole crop was ready, we made little forays and picked a few every now and then. Those were good potatoes and though I used good compost instead of the loose hay mulch next time, thinking I would do even better, I didn't.

I do think however, that it's better to let your potatoes sprout before you plant them. Then you can see if any of them have malformed shoots that could lead to trouble. It is wise, when buying seed potatoes, to check that they are certified virus-free.

Potatoes do not like frost, wet weather or hot nights and when you realize they are close relations of the tomato, eggplant and pepper, it becomes clear why growing them can be a bit trickier than you thought it would be.

They like a loose, sandy loam, a bit on the acid side, and deep and regular mulching.

Bracken is good because it is rich in potassium. Chop it up though.

The mulching takes the place of the "billing" practice favored by the conventional gardener. It is much less trouble and provides the plants with food at the same time.

The slight acidity of the soil—a pH of 5 to 5.5—gives a bit of protection against scab, which spoils the look of the potato.

There are early and main crop varieties. Since the potato has a growing season of four to five months, you can choose a variety suited to the local climate. The local nursery should be able to give advice.

Plant in a sunny spot, 4 inches (10cm) deep and give an all-round space of about 20 inches (50cm) to each plant. During a drought, planting them in a trench about 8-12 inches (20-30cm) deep and covering them with good compost helps, particularly if you water them copiously with comfrey tea and then throw the sludge onto the soil above them.

When the weather is dry, be prepared and make sure the soil at the bottom of the trench is permeable.

Keep up the mulch so that only the top leaves are showing during the whole growing period.

Varieties

Early: Red Pontiac, Red La Soda, Irish Cobbler,

Mid-season: Sutton's Supreme

Late: Kennebec, Katahdin

Main crop: Red Norland, Russet Burbank, Sebago, Viking, Norgold Russet

Pests and Diseases

It is almost quicker to say what they are not susceptible to.

1. Aphids, caterpillars, slugs, snails, wireworms

2. Viral diseases

If the leaves become mottled and the veins yellow, rip out the plant and burn it together with the aphids on it—they probably brought the disease.

Clean up the ground removing every bit of infected material. If you are thorough, you might get away with replanting in the same spot.

3. Blight

If stem and leaves shrivel and there are brown blotches on the leaves, you probably have bacterial blight or potato blight, which is a fungal disease.

To be on the really safe side, rip out and burn the plants and do not use this spot for planting any member of the family for at least 3 years.

4. Gangrene

If you stick a fork into a potato and damage it and leave it in the ground, it will rot.

Good Companions

Peas, Beans, Cabbage, Sweet corn, Broad beans, Nasturtiums, Marigolds

Bad Companions

Apples, Cherries, Cucumber, Pumpkin, Sunflowers, Tomatoes, Raspberry, Rosemary

PUMPKIN

Pumpkin likes warmth, good food and plenty of water. Three or four plants are usually the most an average-sized garden can accommodate. Pumpkins are great travelers; when the vine is about 7 feet (2m) long, it is prudent to pinch out the growing tip to encourage more laterals, which will bear the flowers and fruit.

The flowers are recognizably male and female so, if help in pollination is needed, you will find it easy.

Pumpkins are sensitive and react badly to too much cold, too much heat and too much moisture. They need a long, warm growing season of 5 to 6 months, good soil and regular watering.

The popular way of growing them is to dig out a circle about 20 inches (50cm) in diameter and to pile up the soil round the rim and plant seeds in it, gradually thinning them down to two or three plants by cutting off the unwanted seedlings at ground level to avoid disturbance to those chosen to grow on.

I've never gone to that amount of trouble but just make a few hillocks of good, enriched compost and plant one seed in each of them. Pumpkins germinate easily and quickly and if there is no sign of growth in 6 or 7 days, sow another one. You won't have lost too much time. When the seedling really gets away, I shove scrunched-up chicken wire round it to give it support. I find this easier than having 2 or 3 plants getting themselves entwined with each other. A pumpkin on the rampage is a fine sight with its handsome leaves and strong flowers.

Lifting the vines from the ground to ensure a good air-flow round the leaves is important because they are so prone to mildew—a friend once used an old wire-spring mattress to good effect.

They need a lot of water too—and this is best given in the morning, in case, in spite of your best efforts, you spill water on the leaves. Wet leaves overnight promote mildew.

A weekly dose of liquid manure during the 3.5 to 4 months growing season will be appreciated.

If pushed for space, you could grow a bush pumpkin in a tub or set

THE PRACTICAL ORGANIC GARDENER

one or two out in a bed with 40 inches (100cm) space all round each of them. Don't pick the fruit until the stalk is drying.

Varieties

Connecticut Field, Big Moon, Big Max, Jack-O'-Lantern, Spookie, Small Sugar, Spirit, Lady Godiva

Good Companions

Sweet Corn

Bad Companions

Potatoes

Pests and Diseases

1. Borers
2. Mildew

RADISH

Radish can be grown pretty well all round the year except for the very, very hottest and coldest places. They like a lightish, well-drained soil, some sun, but can cope with partial shade. They are a quick-growing crop—they only take 7 weeks to mature.

In early spring make thin sowings in shallow drills of short rows, about 30 inches (75cm) long. Thin seedlings to 2 inches (5cm) apart when growth is strong. All you have to do now is to keep the soil damp and protected by a light mulch.

Start picking when the radish is small—large ones become woody.

Varieties

Small: Cherry Belle, French Breakfast, Scarlet Globe, Sparkler, Long White Icicle

Large and late: Japanese, Black Spanish, White Chinese, China Rose

Good Companions

Lettuce, Peas, Nasturtiums

Bad Companions

Hyssop

RHUBARB

A rhubarb bed will be productive for several years and turn a spot in the semi-shade into an attractive feature.

It can be grown from seed but most people prefer to buy crowns from a nursery or to cadge a division from a friend.

Rhubarb is hardy—likes well-drained soil rich in humus and a good deep mulch kept around it all through the growing season. The mulch should contain more carboniferous than nitrogenous material or you'll get lush leaves and few fruit stalks. If you think you have cause for worry, sprinkle a little sulfate of potash around each plant. It doesn't like grass near it.

Plant crowns or divisions shallowly about 30 inches (75cm) apart and keep an eye out to see that the soil remains damp enough under the mulch as the plants grow.

Pick the outside fruit stalks and leave the inside ones to grow on. Cut out any flower stalk that appears.

Rhubarb leaves are poisonous to us but are useful for making sprays with which to repel insects.

Varieties

Victoria, Ruby, Valentine, Cherry, Giant Cherry

Pests and Diseases

None to speak of. If you have over-watered, you may get big reddish-brown spots on the leaves. Pick them off and cut down on the water.

SPINACH, ENGLISH

English Spinach only grows well in cool areas. It can only be grown from seed—transplanted seedlings bolt very quickly. Growing plants will bolt if watering or feeding is irregular.

For a supply throughout the winter, sow in autumn, in well-drained slightly alkaline soil, setting 2 or 3 seeds about 4 inches (10cm) deep and 8 inches (20cm) apart.

When growth is established, thin, leaving the strongest plant to grow on.

Mulch well, using predominately green material and add a sprinkling of blood and bone meal every 10 days or so. Water regularly, under the mulch. The plants will appreciate an occasional dose of liquid manure made from nettles, dandelions, comfrey or old dried manure. Some hay or straw around the leaves will keep them clean and dry.

When the leaves are large enough, start picking neatly from the outside. The plants will continue growing and putting out more leaves.

Varieties

Long Standing Bloomsdale, Popeye's Choice, America, Winter Bloomsdale, Melody

Pests and Diseases

1. Aphid
2. Rust

Choose resistant types

Good Companions

Strawberries, Santolina

SUMMER SQUASH

Summer squash is picked when immature. It is more of a bush than a vine. Winter squash is left to ripen on the vine. The skins harden and they are enabled to store well.

Zucchini, a member of the family is listed separately.

The Cucurbit family also includes cucumbers, melons, marrows, gourds and pumpkins so we know what to expect from squash.

They are warm-season plants and hate the cold; they have both male and female plants.

See PUMPKIN for the way to grow them.

Summer squash have large leaves, weak stems, big flowers and fruit that vary in shape. Crookneck, straightneck, pattypan, scallop—the names give an idea of the fruit shape.

The seeds of all types can be sown in spring after the soil has warmed. If you plant before that, they won't germinate. It is probably better to sow them indoors in a tray and to look after them until it is safe to plant them out. You save time that way. When they are obviously starting to grow well, water and mulch well but lightly.

When the first flowers appear, give a weak dose of liquid manure to encourage the plant to put out more.

Pick the fruit while young and small and the skins are tender.

Varieties

Early: Early Prolific Straightneck, Goldbar, Seneca Prolific, White Bush, Early Buttons Hybrid, Green Buttons Hybrid

WINTER SQUASH

Grow in the same way as for Summer Squash but leave much more room around each plant. Don't pick until the winter months.

Varieties

Butternut, Ebony Acorn, Spaghetti Squash, Banana, Green Warted Hubbard, Table Queen, Golden Nugget

Pests and Diseases

1. Bugs, borers and beetles
   Handpick bugs and beetles.

Look for a little hole in the stem to see if borers have got in.

Slit the stem, remove borer and dispose of it. Curve stem over and press into the soil and peg down. You may get a new root from the split.

2. Mildew
3. Bacterial wilt and mosaic virus
   Plant resistant varieties and don't waste time trying to save affected plants. Pull them out and clean up.

Good Companions

Sweet corn

SWEET CORN

Sweet corn is a heavy feeder, likes warm weather and takes from 3 to 5 months to mature, so you can adjust planting time to fit in with the weather in your region.

You can sow the seeds in clumps or blocks or in a trench. If you plant in long single rows, it will make pollination difficult. About 20 plants are usually enough for the average-sized family.

The soil should be slightly alkaline—so a sprinkling of lime before planting is often needed—and there should be plenty of well-rotted organic matter in it and some blood and bone meal or dried chicken pellets.

Sow seed about 1 inch (2-3cm) deep and aim to have plants growing about 12 inches (30cm) apart.

You can make successive sowings about a month apart. Mulch should be deep and can be about a third of the way up the plant stalks. Water regularly and well underneath the mulch.

If bothered by slugs and snails, put down some sawdust to deter them.

Grown in a trench, on pure compost, and given a continuous mulch of rotted leaves and kept well watered, the plants should crop well. When the silks shrivel the cobs should be ready to pick. Save the sulks for use as a coarse mulch.

Varieties

Kandy Korn, White Lightning, Miracle, Golden Bantam, Butter and Sugar

This is a reasonably tough plant not prone to disease or attack by insects.

Good Companions

Broad beans, Potatoes, Melon, Tomatoes, Cucumber, Squash

SWEET POTATO

This plant needs freedom from frost and a soil temperature that doesn't fall below 70°F (20°C) so, if you attempt to grow it in a cooler spot, you will have to take a lot of trouble.

In the right climatic conditions, growth is strong and vigorous and space is needed to accommodate the thrusting vines. A dozen to 15 plants should give an average-sized family a good supply.

Choose some tubers with at least 4 or 5 eyes and leave them to sprout in a dark place or a box of warm sand.

They like a high C:N ratio in the soil so, if you add compost for enrichment, make sure there is far more "brown" than "green" material. Too much nitrogen will make the plants run to leaf at the expense of the tubers.

Plant the sprouted tubers 6 inches (15cm) deep and about 10 inches (25cm) apart with the tops of the shoots just showing above the soil. Water well.

Mulch carefully during growth but don't give the plants any food—again this is to avoid the over-production of leaves. Do not over-water.

It will take about 5 months before the tubers are ready for harvesting. They should be a uniform yellow. Leave in the sun for a day or two to harden before storing.

I don't think there are any varieties.

Pests and Diseases

1. Aphids, caterpillars, cutworms, snails and slugs, wireworms.

2. Fungal diseases
   Plant resistant variety

3. Root-rot

TOMATOES

Tomatoes need sun, a rich, well-drained, slightly acid soil, protection from wind, heavy rain and frost and 3 to 5 months good growing weather.

Most people use bought seedlings. Local knowledge is invaluable, so consult your nursery as to the best variety to buy.

You can get bush tomatoes that don't grow very tall and ones with a twining habit that do, unless you deal with them. You can get those that need stakes and ones that can do without them. There are dwarf tomatoes, mini tomatoes, yellow tomatoes, plum tomatoes, cherry tomatoes, round tomatoes, and egg-shaped ones. Some you grow in the ground, others are best in tubs or pots. There are early, mid-season and late varieties and, if you want a good crop, you have to know how to prune them.

Since they require a rich soil, include plenty of compost in it, but make certain that it isn't too rich in nitrogen or you'll get leafy plants with few fruits. They like plenty of phosphorus. Crushed eggshells and blood and bone meal will help out. In hot areas, the trench method will suit them provided you don't plant them too close together. And make sure you have plenty of comfrey on hand.

Whatever type you choose, give good all-round space when you plant out and, for the tall types, stake each one.

Water the young plants regularly and, when growing well, tie to the stake at about 12-inch (30cm) intervals. Mulch to quite high up the stem to encourage the plants to put out more roots. Nip out any shoots showing between the main stem and the side shoots—you want a clean clear main stem. When there are about 6 or 7 little bunches of fruit showing, pinch out the growing point and a bit of the top growth.

As the fruit grows, do not mind if leaves are keeping the sun off it; it will ripen in the warmth.

Pick the fruit when it is a healthy pink and allow it to finish ripening in a warm place.

Varieties

Early Tall: Early Girl V, Fantastic, Beefmaster VFN, Pixie Hybrid

Main Crop Tall: Better Boy VFN, Burpee's Big Boy, Marglobe VF, Moira, Floramerica

※ Mini: Sweet 100, Yellow Pear, Small Fry VFN, Tiny Tim

Pests and Diseases

1. Aphids, caterpillars, cutworms, fruit fly, slugs and snails, red spider mite, white flies.

2. Verticillium and fusarium wilt. Tobacco mosaic virus.

Remove and destroy affected plants. Do not plant tomatoes or any other member of the Solanum family in this soil for at least 3 years.

3. Blossom-end rot

Spray with comfrey or chamomile tea.

Good Companions

Asparagus, Chervil, Carrot, Celery, Chives, Parsley, Marigolds, Basil

Bad Companions

Rosemary, Potatoes, Fennel, Apricots

TURNIPS AND RUTABAGAS

Both are cool weather crops that can cope with partial shade and need a rich well-drained soil that will not dry out and is not too rich in nitrogen as, though the leaves are edible, the root is the target.

White turnips take 10-12 weeks to come to maturity. Yellow ones—Rutabagas—need 3 to 4 months. By sowing in spring and again in early autumn, you can have two crops a year.

Sow seeds thickly in soil containing plenty of compost or topped with well-rotted mulch. Thin out to 6 inches (15cm) apart and keep the plants well watered as they grow. Mulch generously and give the occasional dose of weak liquid manure.

Varieties

Turnips: All Seasons, White Flat, Shogoin, Tokyo Cross, Just Right, Tokyo Market

Rutabagas: American Purple Top, Laurentian, Long Island Improved, Macomber

Pests and Diseases

Aphids and caterpillars

Good Companions

Peas, Beans, Chives

Bad Companions

Potatoes

ZUCCHINI

Zucchini belong to the same family as cucumber and pumpkin, but make small bushes instead of sprawling growth. They are so useful as cooked vegetables and in salads most people find it worthwhile to grow a dozen plants.

Add compost and/or well-decayed mulch to the soil and plant out seedlings 8 inches (20cm) apart when the soil has become warm in spring. Keep watered and mulched and give the occasional dose of liquid manure. Pick when small.

They only need 2 months or so of warm weather to mature so by staggering planting according to local conditions you can extend picking time.

Varieties

Aristocrat, Ambassador, President Hybrid, Gourmet Globe, Gold Rush

Pests and Diseases

Aphids and caterpillars

Good Companions

Tomatoes, Parsley, Bell Peppers, Swiss chard, Corn